The Beginner's Guide to a

PLANT-BASED
Diet

The Life-Changing Challenge

70+ Recipes

3-week plan

Elizabeth Hayward

Copyright © 2020 by Elizabeth Hayward
All rights reserved. No part of this book may be reproduced or
used in any manner without written permission of the copyright
owner except for the use of quotations in a book review.

TABLE OF CONTENTS

Introduction

Congratulations on purchasing *The Beginner's Guide to Plant-based Diet,* and thank you for doing so.

The following chapters will discuss the fundamental concepts of the plant-based diet to help get you started on your new journey! Before you go turning your life upside down, I want you first to ask yourself why you are doing this in the first place? Do you want to improve your health for yourself? Is it for someone you love? What do you hope to accomplish with a new diet?

These are essential questions to ask yourself because I want you to dedicate your life to yourself. The plant-based diet is so much more than just what you eat. A plant-based diet revolves around making healthy choices and making those choices every day for the rest of your life!

How many times have your diets failed? More than likely, the shortlist started out fantastic. You probably followed it without fault and lost the weight you dreamed of losing. But, after a few months, the rules worked against your social life, so you started giving in here and there and eventually, completely fell off the bandwagon and gained that weight right back.

If you are willing to make a difference in your life, you need to start right now.

Within the chapters of this book, you will find everything you need to know to help you get started. You will find your basic concepts here, tips and tricks to help you get started, and a meal plan at the end of this book to send you on your way.

There are plenty of books on the market on this subject, thank you again for choosing this one! Every effort has been made to ensure that the information is as useful as possible; please enjoy!

THE PLANT-BASED DIET

Chapter 1: Basic Concepts of a Plant-based Diet

When starting any diet, it can be a very confusing time. What can I eat? What am I not supposed to eat? Should I be exercising? Why am I not losing weight?

Luckily for you, this book is going to be your guide every step of the way. You will be handed the information you need, including your basic guidelines for the diet, a thorough list of foods for you to enjoy, and even some delicious recipes to help get you started on your new diet.

You are about to make a lot of significant changes, but with hard work and dedication, you will be reaching your goals in no time! To start this journey off on the right foot, let's go over the basic guidelines you will need to follow as you begin a plant-based diet.

Plant-based 101

In the modern world, there are many diets on the market, so why should a plant-based diet be the one you go with? Two words; Scientific Evidence.

Unlike many other fad diets, there have been years of research studying how plants can benefit our health. The evidence supports that a plant-based diet can boost health and help control, reduce, and sometimes even reverse certain chronic diseases.

The basic concept of a plant-based diet revolves around two primary principles. The first principle is that you will be eating only whole foods. Whole foods are considered natural foods that have not been processed or minimally refined. The second principle is that you will be eating foods that are plant-based. These foods only come from plants and will never include any animal ingredients, including honey, eggs, milk, or meat!

Through a well-rounded plant-based diet, you will be able to eat all of your nutritional needs without being bogged down by the additives included in processed foods and animal products.

Foods You'll Enjoy

Many people become fearful of their diet when they first get started due to the fact that they will no longer be able to enjoy their favorite foods. Luckily on a plant-based diet, there are still some incredible and nutritious foods you will be able to enjoy. Some of the major food categories include:

- **Legumes**
  There are a number of different legumes you will be able to enjoy on the plant-based diet, some you may have never even considered trying! Some of the more popular legumes include lentils, soybeans, kidney beans, chickpeas, black beans, green beans, lima beans, fava beans, black-eyed peas, and more!

- **Whole Grains**
  Up until this point, you may have been eating just white bread. Unfortunately, white bread offers you zero

nutritional value. Now, you can enjoy whole grain foods such as quinoa, wild rice, brown rice, barley, whole what, steel-cut oats, and even amaranth.

- **Roots**
  There is a common misconception that potatoes make people fat. Yes, the French fries you get from the fast-food joint will make you gain weight, but they are drenched in oil! On the plant-based diet, you will be eating whole-foods such as carrots, leeks, potatoes, onions, turnips, beets, radishes, etc.

- **Vegetables**
  On a plant-based diet, you will be able to eat foods that are all colors of the rainbow! If it is grown, you get to enjoy it! Any vegetables such as zucchini, tomatoes, peppers, mushrooms, celery, squash, cauliflower, asparagus will be on your plate on your new diet!

- **Fruits**
  While vegetables are going to make up a significant portion of your new diet, fruits will be another staple. You will enjoy fruits from all different sources such as plums, kiwi, pineapple, mango, cherries, berries, apples, bananas, and apricots. Part of the fun will be eating foods that are in season for the best nutrition and flavors!

The approved foods from the list above will make up a majority of your diet. You may be surprised to learn just how filling and flavor-filled plant-based foods can be. There are also some other foods you will be able to enjoy, but they will need to be kept in moderation. The following foods are healthy, but they are considerably high in fat. If weight loss is one of your goals, you will want to keep the following list to a minimum.

- **Dried Fruit**
- **Seeds**
- **Nuts**
- **Coconut**
- **Avocado**
- **Soy Products**
- **Added Sweeteners**
- **Alcoholic Beverages**

Foods to Avoid

Obviously, following a plant-based diet means avoiding animal products, but there is more to it than that. Up until this point, you have probably been following a SAD diet; Standard American Diet. This diet is filled with dairy, meat, sugar, and oil, and believe it or not; your body has grown addicted to these products. It may be hard to make the switch at first, but eventually, your body will begin craving healthy foods, and you will be able to leave the processed foods behind. Below, you will find a short list of foods you will need to avoid on your new diet.

- **Meat**
  This includes any processed meat, red meat, seafood, or poultry
- **Dairy**
  Cream, Butter, Cheese, Milk, Yogurt, Etc.
- **Eggs**
- **Soda**
- **Fruit Juices**
- **Refined Grains**
  Quick Cook Oats, White Rice, White Flour, White Bread
- **Refined Sugars**

Corn Syrup, White Sugar, Brown Sugar, Cane Sugar, Fructose

As long as you understand the basic concepts of the plant-based diet, you will have no issued getting started. The key is knowing what you can enjoy and work your meals around the whole foods. You will want to set yourself up for success by providing the proper foods in your home, but we will get to that later. For now, it is time to decide what type of plant-based diet is going to work best for you!

Types of Plant-based Diet

Thanks to modern technology, there is a wide variety of food that we get to choose from. Whether you live somewhere, that is hot and humid, or somewhere that it is freezing cold and snowing, more than likely, you have a source that you can get fresh foods from.

While, of course, there is no one "right" way to eat food, you have choices to make. On a plant-based diet, you will not only be improving your health, but you will also be lowering your carbon footprint and decrease animal suffering at the same time. The diet benefits both your health and your conscious!

What it comes down to is what you want for yourself. The best course of action is to educate yourself on the different types of diet out there and decide which is best for your lifestyle, budget, and your body!

Luckily, with the modern market, food sources are more abundant than ever. While this seems like a good thing, the bad side is that many of these foods are less healthy and are filled with preservatives, processed grains, stabilizers, and artificial colors.

All of these additives are useless to the body and can both harm your health and cause you to gain weight! For this reason, a plant-based diet may prove to be most beneficial for your health.

If you have considered going plant-based before, you are not alone! There is a growing number of individuals turning toward a whole food vegetarian diet or even a low-meat diet. If you are ready to commit to a plant-based diet, here you will find several, similar types of plant-based diets that may fit your lifestyle and goals better:

- **Vegetarian**
  A vegetarian diet is the most extensive category when it comes to following a plant-based diet. While most individuals try to avoid meat, seafood, or fish, this diet is pretty flexible. Some vegetarians consider themselves Lacto- or ovo-vegetarian, meaning that they still eat milk and eggs. If these are two products you still consume in your daily life, you may want to consider sticking to a basic vegetarian diet.

- **Vegan**
  A vegan follows a much stricter diet compared to vegetarian, but they are also developing a lifestyle rather than just a diet. Vegans avoid animal products at all costs, including meat, seafood, fish, dairy, honey, eggs, leather, silk, or any clothing made from animals. It is rather strict, but one of the healthier options.

- **Pescatarian**
  If you like eating fish, this will be the best option for you. Pescatarians follow a vegetarian diet, still consuming honey, milk, and other dairy products, but they also eat fish.

- **Flexitarian**
  Finally, we have the flexitarians. These individuals follow a vegetarian diet but are very flexible about the guidelines. Flexitarians generally still consume meat but try to limit their portions. For example, some individuals will only eat meat once or twice a week, and the rest will be plant-based.

At the end of the day, you will need to choose a diet that is going to benefit you the most. It does not matter what other people think of you or what other people think you should be eating. If you want to eat plants to improve your health, that is your choice to make!

If you are not convinced yet, perhaps the next chapter will benefit you. Here, we will be going over all of the incredible ways a plant-based diet will be able to help you improve your life through nutrition. This diet is not just meant to help individuals with weight loss. It is about the environmental impact you can make, the animals you can speak for, and the incredible health benefits that come along the way. It is going to take some extra work, but it will be worth it.

Chapter 2: Benefits of the Plant-based Diet

One of the most important decisions you will ever make for yourself is what diet you should follow. The real question you need to ask yourself is what is important to you? Why should you even follow this diet in the first place?

Before you think about starting a new diet, it is important to realize that whatever you are doing right now obviously isn't working for you. If it were, you wouldn't be here in the first place! Below, you will find yourself some of the reasons that people begin a plant-based diet. Whether you are here for weight loss or health reasons, this diet may be exactly what you are looking for to help change your life for the better.

Weight Loss

When you see the word weight loss, what is the first thing you think of? For many, weight loss includes torturing yourself and starving yourself. Luckily on a plant-based diet, you won't have to endure either!

Society tells us that the only way to lose weight is to restrict your calories, exercise, and be miserable. The truth is that it doesn't have to be the case! On the plant-based diet, there is a major emphasis on foods that low fat and highly nutritious. By eating whole foods, you will be able to shed off all of that excess weight and help prevent health complications that come along with obesity.

Now that food choices have become abundant, obesity has become a serious epidemic. In fact, it is believed that over 69% of adults in the United States are considered obese or overweight! Fortunately, there are lifestyle and diet changes you can make to leave that percentage behind in the dust!

Believe it or not, about 70% of your weight loss is going to come from the diet. Evidence has shown that people taking a plant-based diet will usually have lower BMI and lower risk of cardiovascular disease, high blood pressure, and diabetes, all diseases related to obesity.

Eating the Right Foods
One of the reasons many other diets fail is because the restrictive way of eating is not sustainable! At first, a plant-based diet can come off somewhat hard, but as you get used to eating your new foods, it will become much more manageable. As mentioned earlier, your body is literally addicted to fast food and sugar! The key here is going to be changing your habits. Over time, your body will adapt to craving healthy foods, and you will no longer feel deprived of foods you once thought you could never live without!

Instead of telling yourself that you are limited, you will want to focus on the positive! You should want to eat healthy foods because they are benefiting and fueling you to your fullest potential! The processed foods are meant to fuel you quickly but can harm you in the long run. Now, your diet will help fuel you and keep you healthy!

More Food, Less Calories
The central concept for weight loss is the same for just about any diet. The fewer calories you consume, the more weight you are going to lose! The issue here for other diets is that you most likely

have to starve yourself to get those results. Fortunately for you, that is not true on a plant-based diet.

As you begin to follow your new diet, you will find that calorie counting is going to become a concept of the past. Now, you will be eating foods that are nutrient-dense. Many people are aware of the term nutrient-dense, but they have a hard time applying the concept. Basically, you will be consuming foods that are unprocessed and still packed with their micronutrients and macronutrients.

When you are eating foods that have all the nutrients you need, you will find that you are going to get full faster. Whole foods are naturally lower in calories, so when you fill up faster and eat less, you are automatically taking in fewer calories in a day! By simply cutting out processed foods like refined grains, fast food, and soda, you will begin dropping weight instantly.

Cardiovascular Health

A plant-based diet is one of the healthiest heart diets on the market! The key here is understanding the types and quality of food you are eating on your diet. There was a study performed on 200,000 people to compare their diet choices to their health. It was found that the individuals who ate a plant-based diet seemed to have a lower risk of developing heart disease. This research was compared to individuals who followed a non-plant-based diet.

In the medical world, the term coronary heart disease is used as a general term. Heart disease is a condition where the arteries that are supplying the heart get clogged by a build-up of fat. Once the arteries become completely blocked, this is when individuals are at risk for a heart attack. Sadly, heart disease is one of the world's leading causes of death!

The key concept from this study is the quality of the food you are going to be eating on a plant-based diet. The individuals of this study ate foods, including nuts, legumes, whole-grains, fruits, and vegetables. As you begin your new diet, you will need to learn the difference between healthy plant-based foods and unhealthy ones. Unfortunately, there are plenty of foods that will be labeled "plant-based," including fruit juices, refined grains, and other sugary drinks. While technically, these are "plant-based," they can still potentially lead to a higher risk of heart disease.

Diabetes

Another popular reason people begin a plant-based diet is because it is a very powerful tool in reducing or managing the risk of developing diabetes. While diabetes is a widespread disorder, it is something that could potentially be avoided through diet.

Unfortunately, if you have type 1 diabetes, a plant-based diet may not be the best option for you. Type 1 diabetes is caused in the first place by the failure of the body to make insulin. Type 2 and pre-diabetics, however, can greatly benefit from a plant-based diet. Type 2 Diabetes is caused by the inability of the body to adapt to insulin's effects.

Did you know that about 84.1 million adults in the United States have blood sugar levels that are higher than normal? While they are higher than average, it isn't high enough to be classified as diabetes, making these individuals prediabetic. Typically, these people will not have any symptoms until it is too late. Unfortunately, diabetes is often associated with other issues, such as heart disease.

There was a <u>study</u> done on 200,000 people, and in this study, it was found that individuals who followed a plant-based diet were able to lower their risk of developing diabetes by 34%! In a similar <u>study</u>, it was found that the plant-based diet helped reduce the risk of type 2 diabetes by 50%!

Improve Energy Levels

While following a SAD diet, it isn't uncommon to feel tired and sluggish, especially in the afternoon when the sugar crash hits. The issue with processed foods is that yes, it is quicker and easier to make, but the lack of nutrients means that the energy provided is going to be fast, and the crash is going to come hard!

On a plant-based diet, you will be eating whole foods that will provide you with clean sources of your macronutrients, including protein, carbohydrates, and fats. When you eat the right foods, you will begin to sustain your energy in a natural way. An example of this will be the foods you will be eating that are higher in fiber. Foods that have higher fiber content will help your blood sugar levels increase but then will decrease slow and steady so that you do not experience the sugar crash after.

Another benefit of switching to the plant-based diet is that it will help your digestion process. As you begin to eat more whole foods, your body will begin to function better than ever! Digesting will become easier on your system, and your energy will increase because you are eating foods that are both nutrient-dense and of higher quality compared to the junk you've been shoving in your mouth.

Cognitive Benefits

With age, it seems thoughts leave our head quicker by the day. Could diet be linked to this? Another added benefit for the plant-based diet is the ability to possibly prevent or slow down Alzheimer's disease and cognitive decline in older adults. Studies have found that diets that are higher in antioxidants and plant compounds can typically reverse any cognitive deficits.

On the plant-based diet, you will automatically be increasing the number of vegetables and fruits on your diet. The nutrients found in these foods are highly associated with reducing cognitive decline. In fact, there was a study done on 31,000 people. In this study, it was found that by eating more vegetables and fruits, these individuals were able to reduce their risk of developing dementia and cognitive impairment by 20%.

Environmental Impact

Not only will you gain your wellbeing when you turn to a plant-based diet, but you will also protect the environment. Individuals who follow a plant-based diet will generally leave a smaller environmental footprint. With the world becoming a burning trashcan, every little bit helps.

By adopting a sustainable eating habit, you will, in turn, be consuming less water, reducing the number of greenhouse gas emissions, and also may be able to help reduce the land that is used for factory farming. Unfortunately, it is the factory farming that seems to be the biggest culprit behind environmental degradation and global warming. In fact, studies have shown that if the Western diet shifted to a plant-based pattern, we could reduce greenhouse gas emissions by 70% and water use by 50%. For such a small change, we could create a huge impact to help the whole world!

On a smaller scale, you can make a difference in your own town or city! As you begin a plant-based diet, try shopping for local produce. This can help put money into your local economy and also reduce the reliance on big factory farms. By buying local and organic, you know exactly where your food came from and what is in it. It may take some extra effort, but every little bit helps! After all, we only have one world to live on; why not do your part?

Social Justice

Did you know that on an annual basis, we breed and kill billions of animals for human consumption? If you love animals, you need to stop and ask yourself what the difference is between caring for an animal and killing one for food.

While it is easy enough to create a disconnect from these animals, they are still breathing, living creatures and do not deserve to live or die for our entertainment or convenience. If you are opposed to other forms of discrimination based on physical appearance, class, or sexual orientation, you believe in equality. While, of course, this doesn't mean that humans and animals are the same in every manner, animals do deserve the common decency, and it needs to be recognized that animals should not exist solely to be used for our benefit.

If you are looking to improve your overall health, the plant-based diet is the way to go. It truly is as simple as it seems! If you eat healthy foods, you are going to improve your health. The key takeaway here is that you will need to learn how to build a balanced, plant-based diet to improve your health and hit your goals.

Much like with any other diet, there is no "right" way to do the diet. As you learn more, you will be able to tailor the diet to your lifestyle. As long as you are following the basic concepts of the diet, you will be able to benefit from it. With all of this in mind, it is time to get down to the hard work.

In the chapter to follow, you will be learning everything you need to know to help you get started with your own plant-based diet. Here, you will learn how to create meal plans, how to get enough protein in your diet, and ways to supplement the nutrients you may be missing out on. As you read through, keep your goals in mind to use as motivation on your new, healthy journey!

Chapter 3: Getting Started on a Plant-based Diet

Before you even begin thinking about starting a new diet, it is vital that you set yourself up for success. Many people fail any diet because they fail to make a plan! In the chapter to follow, you will be handed all of the information that you need to help you get started and to help you stick to your diet, even in the difficult times.

The best way to set yourself up for success is to make a meal plan. When you plan your meals for the week, you will have a good idea of how many meals you need to make and if any events are coming up that you will need to plan for. With a meal plan in hand, you will know exactly what you need to buy for the week and what you are going to eat. With a plan, this leaves very little room for failure. So, how do you make a meal plan?

Creating a Meal Plan

The primary issue with most diets is that they are "cookie-cutter" plans. The truth is, there is no one way to follow a diet. For this reason, learning how to create a meal plan is going to be the best way to stick to your new diet! All you will have to do is follow a few simple steps, use some of the delicious recipes provided in this book, and you will be on your merry way of losing, gaining, or even maintaining your weight!

Step One: Nutritional Requirements

The first step you will need to take when developing a meal plan will be determining how many calories you need. This number will range from person to person as it depends upon your height, weight, sex, age, and activity level. If an individual is on the more active side, they will generally need more calories!

If you want to lose weight on your diet, you will need to cut anywhere from 500-750 calories from your diet. By doing this, you will be able to lose about a pound a week. In general, the average calories per day for an adult can be between 1,600 and 3,200 calories per day. You can find your average and subtract from that number by using an online calculator.

Once you have your calorie recommendation in hand, it is time to find the variety and balance to a proper diet. While following a plant-based diet, this should come relatively easy! Your main focus is going to be on fruits, vegetables, nuts, seeds, and whole-grain foods! Through the proper foods, you will be getting all of your recommended vitamins and minerals.

Knowing your macronutrients is going to be important as you make up your meal plan. As you might already know, there is a common misconception that a plant-based diet means you will lack in protein. We will be going over this a bit later, but all you need to know is that it is not true! While following your new diet, you will still have plenty of protein-rich foods such as beans, legumes, nuts, and soy products. Generally, you will want anywhere from 200-700 of your calories coming from a protein source!

Another critical macronutrient to keep in mind is fat. Unfortunately, fat tends to have a bad rep when it comes to diet. On the market, you will see a ton of products labeled "Non-fat" or "Low-Fat." Spoiler alert: these are just as bad for you! The key here is to realize that there are good fats, and they are necessary for a balanced diet. Generally, you will want to keep your fat intake to 30% or less of your total calories. Good fats can come from sources such as olives, soybeans, and nuts. What it comes down to is avoiding trans fats and saturated fats; these are the fats that are associated with diabetes and cardiovascular disease.

Just like with fat, carbohydrates are thought of as an "enemy" for individuals who are trying to lose weight. The truth is, carbohydrates play a crucial role in your health! If you want to provide your body with clean energy, it will be important that you choose the right type of carbs. As you create your meal plan, try your best to choose complex carbs. Complex carbs are whole and unprocessed. Some sources of these carbs include legumes, whole-grain bread, vegetables, and some fruits. It is the simple carbs that you will want to avoid! Anything like white bread, white pasta, or white rice has sugars processed and separated from any nutrients.

As you plan out your meals, you will also want to limit your sugar and salt intake. By cutting processed foods, this will happen mostly automatically, but you will still need to be careful of the salt and sugar when you are cooking your own foods. When you have too much sodium in your diet, this leads to fluid retention. Fluid retention is poor because the risk of stroke, heart disease, and high blood pressure can be increased. Generally, you will want to keep sodium to 2,300 mg a day or less.

Step Two: Make Your Diet Your Own
The problem with many diets is that not one size fits all. We all have different goals, different body types, and completely different lifestyles. For this reason, you will need to set your goals and develop a meal plan around that.

First, you will want to decide how much weight you would like to lose or gain, but remember to keep that goal within a reasonable time frame. On average, a person can safely lose about a pound a week. Drastic weight loss is not only unhealthy but also fairly unachievable. Remember to set goals for yourself that are in your reach. By setting attainable goals this can help motivate you to stick to your diet.

Keep in mind that there is no reason you need to change your habits overnight! If you want to lose weight, you will want to make these changes gradually. One of the best ways to do this is by learning how to slow down your meals. Generally, it takes the brain up to twenty minutes to let your body know that you are full. If you consciously eat slower, you will probably feel full quicker!

Step Three: Creating Your Meals
The final step in creating your own meal plan will be choosing out your meals! If you are just getting started, I highly suggest you try to keep your meal plan as simple as possible. There is absolutely no reason you need to complicate your meals by making separate meals every day of the week!

Instead, consider starting small. If this is your first time, try planning for just breakfast! All you will have to do is take a look at the breakfast recipes provided in this book, choose one or two, and you will be on your way! Once you become more comfortable with the concept of meal planning, you can add more meals to your plan. As you create your meal plans, you will eventually want to include breakfast, lunch, dinner, and some snacks. Luckily, there are many ways to add variety in your meals, so you can really start to get creative!

How to Get Enough Protein

As you begin a plant-based diet, there is one question you will be continuously asked: Where do you get your protein?

Unfortunately, this is due to the fact that there is a lot of misinformation on the subject of protein. While the concern is understandable, it will be no problem for you while following your new diet.

What is Protein?
The real question here is, what is protein, and why is it so important? Protein is one of your three main macronutrients that your body needs for energy. Protein is created from twenty building blocks known as amino acids. These amino acids are important to your body to help build and repair cells.

The most common misconception revolving around protein is how much protein we actually need in our daily diet. The truth is, we only need about 10-15% of daily calories to come from protein, even for individuals who lead an active life. Generally, individuals are able to hit their protein goals without even thinking about it. More than likely, you are already getting more than enough protein in any given diet.

Plant-based Protein Sources
The good news is that while following a plant-based diet, you will be able to get all of the protein you need without any extra effort. Some sources of protein you will want to include in your diet are seeds, nuts, bulgur, legumes, lentils, and beans. As long as you have a well-balanced diet, you should never have an issue getting enough protein in your diet.

Plant-based Staples

When you switch to a plant-based diet, it will require some planning and meal prep. To help set you up for success, you will want to stock your pantry up with some basic staples to help you get started. Over time, you will learn how to use these items for meals and snacks. Below, you will find some basic foods of a plant-based diet.

Legumes

One of the most significant sources of protein on your new diet is going to come from legumes! Legumes are a great staple to have on hand because they offer essential fatty acids, complex carbohydrates, and fiber! Luckily, they are also used in many different kinds of recipes and will fill you right up! Some types of legumes you will want to stock up on include:

- Kidney Beans
- Soybeans
- Pinto Beans
- Edamame
- Chickpeas
- Butter Beans
- Black Beans
- Lentils
- Split Peas
- Lima Beans
- Black-eyed Peas

Whole Grains

As you switch to a plant-based diet, you may find switching your grains is going to be one of the more difficult tasks. In the modern world, white bread and pasta are fairly popular among restaurants and grocery stores. When you begin to make the switch, you will want to make sure your pantry is stocked with minimally processed whole grains. When you eat whole grains, these will provide you with B vitamins and extra fiber in your diet. Some of the best whole grains to stock up on will be:

- Whole Grain Pasta/Flour/Bread/Crackers
- Corn
- Quinoa
- Oats
- Wild Rice
- Brown Rice
- Millet
- Buckwheat

Nuts and Seeds

Nuts and seeds are always great to have on hand, especially if you like to snack! Seeds are very versatile. You can enjoy seeds on or in a number of recipes, whether you are prepping a soup, salad, or even a sandwich! Seeds such as flax and chia seeds will be an excellent source of fatty acids, such as antioxidants, fiber, and omega-3. You can also throw in some pumpkin, sunflower, or sesame seeds when you are looking for a bit of flavor in your recipes!

When you are choosing out nuts for your diet, you will want to look for the packages that are minimally processed and have no salt added. While nuts are loaded with fiber, protein, and healthy fats, these are a food item you will want to keep to a minimum as there is such thing as too much good fat! You will want to consider healthier options, such as:

- Walnuts
- Hazelnuts
- Cashews
- Almonds

Seasonings and Condiments

The secret to any proper diet is to add the spice of variety! As you stock your pantry, you will want to load up on the seasonings and plant-based condiments to keep your meals full of flavor. Whether you like it sweet or spicy, you will want the ability to do both. Below, you will find some popular items to keep on hand.

- Thyme
- Oregano
- Paprika
- Turmeric
- Cinnamon
- Cumin
- Mustard
- Balsamic Vinegar
- Apple Cider Vinegar
- Vegetable Stock

Plant-based Alternatives

When people first switch over to a plant-based diet, they are afraid that they will never be able to enjoy their favorite foods ever again. While this is slightly true, the good news is that there are plenty of plant-based alternatives to help the transition become a bit easier.

Milk and Egg Alternatives

Luckily, the popularity of the plant-based diet is growing by the day! Local stores are beginning to offer a number of different non-dairy milks such as almond, hempseed, coconut, cashew, and rice milk. These kinds of milk are easy to substitute in any recipe and still use the same measurements.

An egg is another ingredient people feel they cannot live without, especially if they like to bake. The good news is that there are several options for you to try. Each of the following recipes is equivalent to one egg:

- ¼ Cup of Pureed Banana
- 3 Tablespoons of Ground Flax Seed and 6 Tablespoons of Water
- ¼ Cup of Unsweetened Apple Sauce

Cheese and Meat Alternatives

You may not believe it, but many people are addicted to cheese! Generally, cheese is one of the most challenging items for people to give up when they begin a plant-based diet. When you are first starting the diet, you can try blended cashews, nutritional yeast, or sliced avocado if you are looking for a creamy texture or a cheesy taste. These are excellent to add to anything from sandwiches to tacos.

As far as store-bought cheeses go, you will want to be careful. Many of the non-cheeses on the market are over-processed soy products. If you really need something that is closely related to cheese, you will want to look for the Daiya brand. Daiya is becoming more popular, and their products are not soy-based.

The same rule goes for mock meats. Unfortunately, when you find textured vegetable protein, these are a byproduct of soybean oil. While there are lots of "meatless meats" on the market and they are technically plant-based, they have loads of additives. In general, you will want to stick to whole foods and leave these fake products out of your diet.

Making Healthier Lifestyle Choices

While eating your fruits and vegetables is going to be necessary, good health will require making healthier lifestyle choices. As you begin to change your habits to healthier ones, it can help you gain energy, focus, happiness, and it could help you live longer! Below, you will find some simple lifestyle changes you may want to consider. Some of them may seem small, but when added to the proper schedule of diet and exercise, it can lead to vast improvements

Sleep

Most people genuinely underestimate how important sleep is. Generally, people need anywhere from six to nine hours of sleep every night. If you skip even one hour, your risk of obesity will increase by 23%! You can improve your sleep quality by creating a schedule for yourself and a comfortable environment to sleep in. If those don't do the trick, you will want to consider essential oils or sleep sounds to help you fall asleep quicker and deeper.

Stay Hydrated

Another meaningful lifestyle change is learning how to stay hydrated! Ideally, you will want to drink at least eight eight-ounce glasses of water per day. When you stay hydrated, this can help you lose weight, gain energy, and improve skin. For some, this may seem like a small change, but it really can work wonders for your whole body.

Stay Active

On your new diet, you may find that you have much more energy than when you were following a SAD diet. Now, this doesn't necessarily mean you need to go for an hour to the gym and lift weights, but you're going to want to try moving your body at least a few days a week. When you pair exercise with the proper diet, you will lose weight faster than you would if you just focus on diet. Luckily, there are plenty of activities for you to try, whether it be spinning, dancing, or going for a stroll around your neighborhood.

When you combine these lifestyle choices with your new diet, watch out world! It is going to be a whole new, healthier version of you.

Tips for Eating Out

When starting a new diet, it may seem next to impossible to eat out at any restaurant. To help you along the way, use the following tips when you are out at a restaurant.

• Ask for Accommodations

One way or another, there is always a way to eat plant based. You can try to eat more plant-based by asking to leave cream sauce off or substituting meat for a vegetable.

• Eat Before you Go

If you are nervous about eating out at a restaurant, try to eat before you head out. Even if you just have a bowl of rice, it can hold you over so you can have a small salad at the restaurant.

• Get Creative

Last, but not least, you will have to learn how to get creative with your meals. Just because something is not on the menu, doesn't mean you can't ask for it. You can even try making a meal out of side dishes. If you are truly dedicated to this lifestyle, there is always a way!

Common Mistakes on a Plant-based Diet

As a beginner, you are bound to make some mistakes, and that is okay! The important thing is to take your mistakes in stride and keep pushing forward. While it may seem challenging at first to create a well-rounded diet, you can prepare yourself for the worst by learning the common mistakes most people make when they are first starting. By knowing the common mistakes, you can avoid them before they even happen!

Vegan/ Vegetarian Does Not Mean Healthier

With the plant-based diet growing in popularity, many companies have started to label their foods "vegan" and "vegetarian." Unfortunately, this label does not automatically make the food healthier for you. In fact, many soy-based products, such as meat alternatives and veggie burgers, are highly processed and have a large number of artificial ingredients. To stay on the safe side, you will want to leave these types of foods out of your diet.

Eating Too Few Calories

As mentioned earlier, people who begin eating a plant-based diet will automatically be consuming fewer calories. While this can be beneficial for weight loss, getting enough calories will be very important for your overall health. Your body relies on calories and needs the energy to function properly. When you limit your calories too much, it could lead to a slower metabolism, fatigue, and other nutrient deficiencies.

Lacking in Vitamin B12

You may not realize it, but Vitamin B12 plays several important roles in creating red blood cells and DNA. The issue with a plant-based diet is that many sources of vitamin B12 are found in animal products, including milk, eggs, poultry, and meat. When you are not eating any of these products, it can lead to a deficiency in B12. Some of the popular side effects include numbness, anemia, memory issues, and fatigue. To help combat this deficiency, you will want to consider taking a supplement along with a balanced diet.

Lacking in Iron

The lack of iron will be one of the pitfalls of a plant-based diet. Plant sources of iron are non-heme. Essentially, this just means that your body is going to have a hard time absorbing this type of iron. Due to this fact, plant-based individuals put themselves at risk for anemia and could suffer from symptoms such as dizziness, shortness of breath, and fatigue. In order to combat this, you can eat sources that are higher in iron, such as oats, seeds, nuts, beans, and lentils. You'll want to combine them with foods high in vitamin C along with these foods. Vitamin C can help your body absorb non-heme iron.

Lacking in Omega-3 Fatty Acids

Another essential part of your diet is going to be Omega-3 fatty acids. While the most common sources of omega-3 fatty acids are fatty fish and fish oil, that does not mean that you are out of luck while following a plant-based diet. Instead, you will want to consider a supplement of algal oil or enjoy foods, including walnuts, chia seeds, hemp seeds, and flaxseeds.

The bottom line is that all of these mistakes can be avoided. It is going to take some extra effort, but it will be worth it. As long as you make a plan, you will be setting yourself up for success!

The next step of starting a plant-based diet is going to be learning some of the delicious recipes you will get to enjoy. In the following few chapters, you will be provided with some recipes for breakfast, lunch, dinner, and even some dessert. Remember that as long as you are eating whole foods, you are on the right path!

MEASUREMENT CONVERSION CHART

Liquid (Fluid or Volume) Measurements (approximate):

1 teaspoon equals		1/3 tablespoon	5 ml
1 tablespoon	1/2 fluid ounce	3 teaspoons	15 ml
2 tablespoons	1 fluid ounce	1/8 cup, 6 teaspoons	30 ml
1/4 cup	2 fluid ounces	4 tablespoons	59 ml
1/3 cup	2 2/3 fluid ounces	5 tablespoons + 1 teaspoon	79 ml
1/2 cup	4 fluid ounces	8 tablespoons	118 ml
2/3 cup	5 1/3 fluid ounces	10 tablespoons + 2 teaspoons	158 ml
3/4 cup	6 fluid ounces	12 tablespoons	177 ml
7/8 cup	7 fluid ounces	14 tablespoons	207 ml
1 cup	8 fluid ounces / 1/2 pint	16 tablespoons	237 ml
2 cups	16 fluid ounces / 1 pint	32 tablespoons	473 ml
4 cups	32 fluid ounces	1 quart	946 ml
1 pint	16 fluid ounces/ 1 pint	32 tablespoons	473 ml
2 pints	32 fluid ounces	1 quart	946 ml, 0.946 liters
8 pints	1 gallon/ 128 fluid ounces		3785 ml, 3.78 liters
4 quarts	1 gallon/ 128 fluid ounces		3785 ml, 3.78 liters
1 liter	1.057 quarts		1000 ml
1 gallon	128 fluid ounces		3785 ml, 3.78 liters

Dry (Weight) Measurements (approximate):

1 ounce		30 grams (28.35 g)
2 ounces		55 grams
3 ounces		85 grams
4 ounces	1/4 pound	125 grams
8 ounces	1/2 pound	240 grams
12 ounces	3/4 pound	375 grams
16 ounces	1 pound	454 grams
32 ounces	2 pounds	907 grams

Oven Temperature Conversions:

Farenheit	Celsius
275° F	140° C
300° F	150° C
325° F	165° C
350° F	180° C
375° F	190° C
400° F	200° C
425° F	220° C
450° F	230° C
475° F	240° C

THE 70+ DELICIOUS RECIPES!

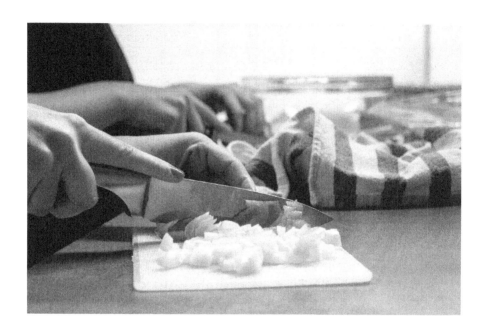

Measurement Keys

Measurement	Abbreviation
Cup	C.
Tablespoon	T.
Teaspoon	t.

PLEASE NOTE: Nutritional Values are Per Serving

Chapter 4: Breakfast

Espresso Breakfast Bowl

Prepping: 5 Minutes
Cooking: 10 Minutes
Servings: 1

Calories: 300
Carbs: 50g
Fats: 10g
Proteins: 10g

Ingredients
- Banana (1/3, Sliced)
- Almond Milk (1/2 C.)
- Rolled Oats (1 C.)
- Blueberries (3 T.)
- Chia Seeds (1 t.)
- Peanut Butter (2 t.)
- Espresso (1/2 C.)

Directions
1. Breakfast bowls are a great way to start the day, especially this one that has a boost of caffeine! You will want to start this recipe off by mixing the rolled oats with the almond milk and the espresso. You can either cook the rolled oats in these ingredients or refrigerate everything overnight.
2. When you are ready to serve your bowl, top with the blueberries, peanut butter, and sliced banana pieces. For

a bit of texture, sprinkle your chia seeds over the top and enjoy your breakfast.

Banana Breakfast Cookies

Prepping: 5 Minutes
Cooking: 30 Minutes
Servings: 6

Calories: 150
Carbs: 30g
Fats: 5g
Proteins: 5g

Ingredients
- Bananas (2, Mashed)
- Old-fashioned Oatmeal (1 ½ C.)
- Vanilla Extract (1 t.)
- Chopped Walnuts (1/4 C.)
- Cinnamon (1 t.)
- Raisins (1/3 C.)
- Applesauce (1 C.)

Directions
1. Cookies for breakfast? On the plant-based diet, you can! Begin this recipe by prepping the oven to 350.
2. As this warms up, you will want to get out your mixing bowl and add in your applesauce, cinnamon, and vanilla extract. Once these are in place, you will want to add in the rest of your ingredients and create a dough.
3. When your dough is all set, take out a cookie sheet and line it with parchment paper. Once this is in place, drop spoonful's of the batter onto the sheet and then pop the dish into the oven for about thirty minutes. By the end of this time, the cookies should begin to look golden.

4. Finally, allow the cookies to rest for about five minutes until breakfast is ready.

Basic Breakfast Hash Browns

Prepping: 5 Minutes
Cooking: 15 Minutes
Servings: 4

Calories: 150
Carbs: 20g
Fats: 10g
Proteins: 5g

Ingredients
- Baking Potatoes (1 Pound)
- Salt (to Taste)
- Olive Oil (3 T.)
- Pepper (to Taste)

Directions
1. While there are many ways to make a potato, there is something about being able to make a nice, crispy hash brown. Before you think about cooking, you will want to take some time to peel and grate all of your potatoes.
2. Once the potatoes are grated, work in batches to squeeze the moisture out of the potato. The best way to complete this task is with a potato ricer or lemon press. If you don't have either of these products, a good old-fashioned paper towel will do the trick. This step is key for creating crunchy hash browns instead of mushy ones.
3. Next, it is time to cook your potatoes. Heat the skillet over medium heat and put the oil in it. Once the olive oil heats up, add in the grated potatoes and add salt and pepper to your liking.

4. After three minutes, you will want to gently lift up an edge of the potato to see if they are golden or not. If they are a golden-brown color, carefully use two spatulas to help flip the potatoes all at once.
5. Once you have cooked on the other side, remove the pan from the stovetop, and your hash browns will be set.

Spinach and Carrot Cakes

Prepping: 10 Minutes
Cooking: 15 Minutes
Servings: 4

Calories: 130
Carbs: 30g
Fats: 5g
Proteins: 5g

Ingredients

- Onion (1/2, Chopped)
- Spinach (1/2 C., Chopped)
- Potatoes (3, Grated)
- Carrot (1/2, Grated)
- Salt (to Taste)
- Corn Flour (1 ½ T.)
- Chili Powder (1/2 t.)

Directions

1. This recipe is for a healthier alternative to pancakes. To begin, you will want to get out a mixing bowl and gently mix together the chopped and grated vegetables. Once they are well combined, add in a little bit of salt and mix again.
2. With all of your veggies in place, you will want to take a few moments to squeeze any excess moisture out. When this step is complete, add in the cornflour, chili powder, and a little bit more salt to your own taste. Now that you have your mixture, use your hands and create patties.
3. You'll want to get your skillet out and position it over medium heat until your patties are all prepared. When

the pan gets hot, you can add some olive oil to the pan and place the patties in the oven.

4. You are going to go ahead and cook the patties on both sides for four or five minutes. The patties should be cooked through by this time and slightly browned. Once they are done, serve hot!

Cinnamon Roll Oats

Prepping: 8 Hours
Cooking: 0 Minutes
Servings: 5

Calories: 200
Carbs: 30g
Fats: 5g
Proteins: 5g

Ingredients
- Almond Milk (2 ½ C.)
- Rolled Oats (2 ½ C.)
- Ground Cinnamon (1 t.)
- Vanilla Extract (2 t.)
- Brown Sugar (8 t.)

Directions
1. While generally, you will want to keep your sugar intake to a minimum, it is okay to splurge every once in a while! To make this recipe, you will want to get out a cup or mason jar.
2. Once you have your jar out, add in all of the ingredients from the list above and stir together really well.
3. Now that the jar is set, you are going to place it in the fridge overnight. This way, you will have a delicious and sweet breakfast to look forward to the next day!

Crumble Apple Muffins

Prepping: 10 Minutes
Cooking: 30 Minutes
Servings: 4

Calories: 450
Carbs: 60g
Fats: 10g
Proteins: 10g

Ingredients
- Almond Meal (1/2 C.)
- Rolled Oats (1/2 C.)
- Brown Rice Flour (1 C.)
- Almond Milk (1 C.)
- Coconut Sugar (1/2 C.)
- Flaxseed Meal (2 T.)
- Baking Powder (1 t.)
- Vanilla (1 t.)
- Banana (1, Mashed)
- Apple (1, Diced)
- Cardamom (1/8 t.)
- Almond Meal (2 T.)
- Coconut Sugar (2 T.)

Directions
1. While muffins do take a little bit of extra effort, they will be excellent to have when you are strapped for time and need to grab something quick and healthy. Before you begin this recipe, you will want to prep your oven to 350 and take out your muffin pan and line each well.

2. Next, you will want to take the time to peel and dice the apples. Once this step is completed, set the apples to the side and get out another bowl.

3. In this other bowl, you will make the topping for the muffins. Simply combine the almond meal, coconut sugar, and the cinnamon. Once this is done, set this to the side as well.

4. Now, it is time to make the muffin base! In a large bowl, you will want to mix together the flaxseed meal, almond meal, rolled oats, coconut sugar, and the brown rice flour. Once these are combined fairly well, add in your mashed banana, vanilla extract, and the almond milk.

5. Last, you are going to want to fold in the apple pieces you diced earlier. Once this is ready, carefully spoon the batter into the muffin liners and then gently sprinkle the topping over each muffin.

6. When you are ready to make your muffins, pop the dish into the oven for about thirty minutes. At the end of this time, you should be able to poke the muffins with a fork and have it come out clean. If they are cooked the way you like them, remove the dish from the oven and allow it to cool.

Plant-based Omelet

Prepping: 5 Minutes
Cooking: 20 Minutes
Servings: 1

Calories: 250
Carbs: 30g
Fats: 10g
Proteins: 25g

Ingredients
- Nutritional Yeast (2 T.)
- Silken Tofu (3/4 C.)
- Onion (1/4 C., Chopped)
- Mushrooms (1/4 C., Chopped)
- Spinach (1/4 C., Chopped)
- Cornstarch (1 t.)
- Salt (to Taste)
- Hummus (2 T.)
- Paprika (1/4 t.)
- Pepper (to Taste)

Directions
1. Omelets are a classic breakfast favorite. This plant-based alternative is going to be just as delicious! Before you begin cooking, you will want to prep the oven to 375.
2. As the oven heats up, you will want to take a few moments to prep your vegetables and drain your tofu of any excess moisture.
3. You'll want to start heating a skillet over medium heat when you're finished. Once it is warm, add in some olive oil and begin cooking your vegetables. When your

vegetables are cooked through, remove them from the heat and set to the side.

4. As the vegetable cook, you will want to add the tofu, cornstarch, hummus, nutritional yeast, and seasonings into a food processor and blend. If needed, you may have to add some water to help thin out the mixture.

5. When you are ready to make the omelet, you will want to coat the skillet pretty well and then spoon some batter into the bottom. As it cooks, carefully add the vegetables to half of the top like you would with a regular omelet.

6. Go ahead and cook the omelet for about five minutes or until the edges begin to dry. Once it looks fairly cooked through, you will want to place the skillet into the oven and cook for about fifteen minutes. If you like your omelet a bit harder, you will want to leave it in for a little longer.

7. When you are set to serve the omelet, gently fold the omelet and dish some more cooked vegetables over the top. Season with some more salt and pepper and then enjoy!

Scrambled Tofu

Prepping: 5 Minutes
Cooking: 20 Minutes
Servings: 2

Calories: 150
Carbs: 5g
Fats: 10g
Proteins: 15g

Ingredients
- Olive Oil (1/2 T.)
- Nutritional Yeast (1 T.)
- Extra-firm Tofu (1/2 Block)
- Garlic Clove (1, Minced)
- Ground Cumin (1/8 t.)
- Salt (to Taste)

Directions
1. For breakfast with a boost of protein, this tofu scramble is going to be perfect for you! To get going, you want to heat up your olive oil over medium heat in a skillet. As the pan warms up, go ahead and break your firm tofu into chunks.
2. When you are set to cook your scrambled tofu, add the garlic and tofu into the pan and cook for five minutes or so on either side. At the end of this time, the tofu should be fairly golden. As the tofu cooks, feel free to break it up as much as you would like!
3. Once the tofu is cooked to your liking, you can then add in the cumin and the nutritional yeast. Once the tofu absorbs the nutritional yeast, remove from heat and serve up your breakfast, warm!

Sweet Coconut Breakfast Bowl

Prepping: 5 Minutes
Cooking: 0 Minutes
Servings: 1

Calories: 400
Carbs: 50g
Fats: 25g
Proteins: 5g

Ingredients
- Apple (1, Chunked)
- Shredded Coconut (2 T.)
- Medjool Dates (2, Chopped)
- Almond Butter (1 Tablespoon)
- Pecans (2 T.)

Directions
1. While this recipe is on the simpler side, it is delicious! You will begin this recipe by taking out your food processor and combining the coconut, pecans, apple pieces, and the dates. Once it is mixed together well, you can place it in your serving bowl.
2. For a final touch, melt some almond butter in the microwave and stir it into your apple mixture.
3. When you are set to serve, sprinkle some pecans over the top and enjoy.

Raspberry Energy Balls

Prepping: 5 Minutes
Cooking: 0 Minutes
Servings: 14

Calories: 50
Carbs: 10g
Fats: 4g
Proteins: 3g

Ingredients
- Almond Flour (1 C.)
- Rolled Oats (2 C.)
- Shredded Coconut (1/4 C.)
- Frozen Raspberries (1 C.)
- Raisins (7 T.)

Directions
1. These energy balls are easy to make and will be a perfect breakfast when you are on the run! All you need to do is take all the ingredients and place them in a food processor. Save half of the shredded coconut for later as you do this. Then, go ahead and blend the ingredients until everything is smooth.
2. Now that you have your mixture roll the dough into balls and carefully roll through coconut until the balls are well coated. Once this is complete, place them into the fridge and allow to solidify for at least twenty minutes before eating.

Chapter 5: Smoothies and Drinks

Green Machine Smoothie

Prepping: 5 Minutes
Cooking: 0 Minutes
Servings: 2

Calories: 150
Carbs: 50g
Fats: 0g
Proteins: 5g

Ingredients
- Spinach (1 C.)
- Pear (1/2, Chopped)
- Cucumber (1/2, Chopped)
- Pineapple (1/2, Chopped)
- Mint Leaves (10, Chopped)
- Lime (1)
- Agave (1 t.)

Directions
1. For a smoothie packed to the brim with greens, place all of the ingredients into your blender and then carefully squeeze the juice from the lime over the top.
2. Once these items are in place, add some crushed ice in and blend until smooth. When you have reached a consistency of your liking, pour, and serve your smoothie.

Good Morning Detox Smoothie

Prepping: 10 Minutes
Cooking: 0 Minutes
Servings: 4

Calories: 120
Carbs: 30g
Fats: 2g
Proteins: 5g

Ingredients
- Coconut Water (1 C.)
- Orange Juice (1 C.)
- Raspberries (2 C.)
- Ginger Root (3 Inches)
- Kale (1 C.)
- Mango (1 C., Chopped)
- Lemon Juice (2 T.)

Directions
1. Every once in a while, a good detox smoothie is great for the system. You can make this smoothie by place all of the ingredients above into your blender and pulse for thirty seconds or until smooth.

Chia Berry Smoothie

Prepping: 10 Minutes
Cooking: 0 Minutes
Servings: 6

Calories: 150
Carbs: 30g
Fats: 5g
Proteins: 2g

Ingredients
- Strawberries (2 C.)
- Raspberries (2 C.)
- Blackberries (2 C.)
- Banana (2)
- Water (2 C.)
- Chia Seeds (1/4 C.)
- Agave (4 T.)

Directions
1. This smoothie has a number of benefits, including fiber, protein, manganese, calcium, potassium, and some vitamin C. If you are feeling a little under the weather, this smoothie should do the trick!
2. When you are set to make your smoothie, place everything into your blender and pulse for thirty seconds or until smooth. Once it is set, pour into your glass and drink up.

Sunrise Smoothie

Prepping: 5 Minutes
Cooking: 0 Minutes
Servings: 1

Calories: 300
Carbs: 50g
Fats: 2g
Proteins: 5g

Ingredients
- Mango (1/2 C.)
- Raspberries (1/2 C.)
- Pineapple (1/2 C.)
- Banana (1)
- Coconut Water (1 C.)
- Lemon Juice (2 T.)

Directions
1. To make this beautiful smoothie, you will want to take all of the ingredients from the list above and blend in your blender for thirty seconds or until smooth.
2. If you are looking for presentation, you will want to blend the raspberries with a little bit of the water and layer your smoothie to look like a sunset or a sunrise!

Oatmeal and Berry Smoothie

Prepping: 5 Minutes
Cooking: 0 Minutes
Servings: 2

Calories: 200
Carbs: 30g
Fats: 5g
Proteins: 5g

Ingredients
- Banana (1)
- Rolled Oats (1/2 C.)
- Almond Milk (1 C.)
- Vanilla Extract (1/2 t.)
- Strawberries (14, Chopped)
- Agave (1 t.)

Directions
1. This recipe is a bit different, but the strawberries give a nice touch of sweetness for any breakfast smoothie. You're going to make this smoothie by popping all the ingredients into your blender and mixing up for about 30 seconds. By the end, the oats should be mixed in well and can be enjoyed immediately.

Creamy Orange Smoothie

Prepping: 10 Minutes
Cooking: 0 Minutes
Servings: 2

Calories: 280
Carbs: 60g
Fats: 4g
Proteins: 5g

Ingredients
- Almond Milk (1 C.)
- Orange (2)
- Banana (2)
- Vanilla Extract (1/2 t.)

Directions
1. If you enjoyed orange creamsicles growing up, this smoothie is going to be right up your ally! To make this delicious smoothie, simply take all of the ingredients from the list above and place it into your blender.
2. When everything is in place, blend or pulse on high for thirty seconds before pouring and enjoying your morning smoothie.

PBC Breakfast Smoothie

Prepping: 5 Minutes
Cooking: 0 Minutes
Servings: 2

Calories: 350
Carbs: 40g
Fats: 20g
Proteins: 15g

Ingredients
- Cocoa Powder (2 T.)
- Peanut Butter (1/4 C.)
- Almond Milk (1 C.)
- Banana (1)
- Vanilla Extract (1/2 t.)

Directions
1. Sometimes, we need a touch of sweetness for breakfast! In this smoothie, the peanut butter, banana, and chocolate create a perfect blend that isn't too sweet!
2. To make this smoothie, place everything into your blender and blend on high for thirty seconds. If you like your smoothie on the thicker side, feel free to add in some ice before serving.

The Fat Burner

Prepping: 10 Minutes
Cooking: 0 Minutes
Servings: 4

Calories: 10
Carbs: 1g
Fats: 0g
Proteins: 0g

Ingredients

- Water (12 Oz.)
- Lemon Juice (1 Tablespoon)
- Apple Cider Vinegar (2 T.)
- Stevia (1/2 t.)
- Ground Cinnamon (1 t.)

Directions

1. As you learned earlier, it is vital that you stay hydrated on any diet you choose to follow. With this detox water, you will be able to stay hydrated and boost your metabolism at the same time.
2. To create this fat-burning water, you will just have to get out a glass and add in all of the ingredients from the list above. This can be served immediately or placed in the fridge for later.

Virgin Mango Coladas

Prepping: 10 Minutes
Cooking: 0 Minutes
Servings: 4

Calories: 300
Carbs: 40g
Fats: 5g
Proteins: 2g

Ingredients
- Coconut Milk (1 Can)
- Mango (2 C., Pureed)
- Pineapple (5 C., Diced)
- Ice

Directions
1. Sometimes, a nice mocktail is a wonderful way to end the day. If you need something a little stiffer, feel free to add in your own rum! To begin this drink, you will want to place the mango into a food processor and puree until it is smooth. Once this is done, you will pour the mango into the bottom of your serving glass.
2. Next, pop the pineapple, coconut milk, and some ice into your blender and blend until smooth. Once this is set, pour over your pureed mango and enjoy your beverage.

Sweet Watermelon Lemonade

Prepping: 10 Minutes
Cooking: 0 Minutes
Servings: 4

Calories: 150
Carbs: 40g
Fats: 0g
Proteins: 1g

Ingredients
- Water (1/2 C.)
- Watermelon (4 C., Cubed)
- Sugar (1/2 C.)
- Lemon Juice (1 C.)

Directions
1. This beverage is both sweet and tangy, making it incredibly refreshing on those hot summer days! If you're ready for some watermelon lemonade, you'll want to smooth all the ingredients in your blender and puree.
2. When this is all set, you can pour into your serving glasses and enjoy. For a little garnish, save some of the watermelon pieces to throw into your drink.

Chapter 6: Salads, Soups, and Side Dishes

Quinoa and Apple Salad

Prepping: 5 Minutes
Cooking: 20 Minutes
Servings: 6

Calories: 250
Carbs: 40g
Fats: 10g
Proteins: 5g

Ingredients
- Cooked Quinoa (2 C.)
- Carrots (2 C., Chopped)
- Apple (2 C., Chopped)
- Mixed Greens (3 C.)
- Apple Chutney (1/3 C.)
- Parsley (1/4 C.)
- Walnuts (1/2 C., Chopped)

Directions
1. Before you assemble your salad, you will want to take the time to cook your quinoa ahead of time and chop up your fruits and vegetables according to the ingredient instructions.
2. When you are set to make your salad, toss everything into a bowl, and your salad will be set to be served.

The Ultimate Crunch Salad

Prepping: 30 Minutes
Cooking: 0 Minutes
Servings: 10

Calories: 150
Carbs: 5g
Fats: 10g
Proteins: 1g

Ingredients
- Radishes (1 C.)
- Cucumbers (2 C.)
- Cabbage (1 C., Shredded)
- Olive Oil (1/2 C.)
- White Wine Vinegar (6 T.)
- Dill (1/2 C.)

Directions
1. This salad is a bit out of the ordinary, but it can be very refreshing on warmer days. To begin making this salad, you will first want to slice up the cucumbers and radishes. Once this is completed, place it into a mixing bowl along with the shredded cabbage.
2. Now that all is in order, drizzle the olive oil, vinegar, and dill gently over the top and mix very well.
3. Once all the ingredients are covered, you'll want to place the dish in the fridge for at least thirty minutes to allow all the flavors to soak in. When this step is complete, you are set to serve your crunchy salad.

Spicy Quinoa Baked Salad

Prepping: 10 Minutes
Cooking: 30 Minutes
Servings: 4

Calories: 450
Carbs: 60g
Fats: 10g
Proteins: 15g

Ingredients
- Garlic Cloves (3, Minced)
- Black Beans (1 Can)
- Corn (1 C.)
- Red Bell Pepper (1 C., Diced)
- Yellow Bell Pepper (1 C., Diced)
- Olive Oil (1 T.)
- Onion (1, Chopped)
- Cilantro (1 T.)
- Cayenne Pepper (1/4 t.)
- Cumin (1/4 t.)
- Nutritional Yeast (1/2 C.)
- Cooked Quinoa (1 C.)

Directions
1. Yes, a baked salad! To begin this recipe, you can go ahead and cook the quinoa according to the directions on the package and also prep your oven to 350.
2. Once the quinoa is cooked, you will want to set that to the side and get out another skillet to place over medium heat. As the skillet warms up, you will want to add in the olive oil, garlic, and onion. Go ahead and cook these

ingredients until the onion is soft or for about five minutes.

3. When the onion is cooked to your liking, add in the rest of the vegetables and spices. With everything in place, cook these ingredients for another six or seven minutes. By the end, your veggies should be nice and tender.

4. Next, you will want to get out a casserole dish. Here, you will want to throw in the cooked quinoa and your freshly cooked vegetables. With these in place, add the nutritional yeast and chopped cilantro on top and then place the dish into the oven for about fifteen minutes.

5. Remove the dish from the oven after fifteen minutes and allow to cool before serving.

Cucumber and Chickpea Salad

Prepping: 10 Minutes
Cooking: 0 Minutes
Servings: 4

Calories: 180
Carbs: 30g
Fats: 5g
Proteins: 5g

Ingredients
- Olive Oil (1 T.)
- Lemon Juice (2 T.)
- Tomato (1 C., Diced)
- Onion (1/2 C., Diced)
- Cucumber (2 C., Diced)
- Chickpeas (1 Can)
- Parsley (1/2 T.)

Directions
1. While this salad may seem to be on the simpler side, there is nothing simple about these flavors! Before you build your salad, take some time to dice up the vegetables according to the directions.
2. Once your veggies are set, add them into a salad bowl and mix well with the lemon juice and olive oil. For a final touch, sprinkle some fresh parsley over the top and enjoy your salad.

Roasted Avocado and Carrot Salad

Prepping: 5 Minutes
Cooking: 30 Minutes
Servings: 4

Calories: 180
Carbs: 15g
Fats: 15g
Proteins: 3g

Ingredients

- Avocado (1/2, Sliced)
- Olive Oil (3 T.)
- Lemon (1/2, Juiced)
- Cumin (1/4 t.)
- Carrots (2 C., Sliced)
- Salt (to Taste)

Directions

1. Sometimes, you want a recipe that is a little different! While this salad is only made with a few ingredients, it is perfect as a base or a side dish. To begin, prep your oven to 400.
2. As the oven warms up, you will want to take some time to chop your carrots up and toss them in the cumin and olive oil. If you would like, you can also season with pepper and salt.
3. Next, you will want to lay the carrots out onto a baking sheet lined with foil. With this in place, you will want to pop the dish into the oven for about twenty minutes. Once they are roasted properly, remove them from the oven.

4. Now, add the carrots into a serving bowl along with the avocado slices and gently squeeze your half of a lemon over the top. If you want, just add some extra salt and pepper and enjoy it!

Basic Cauliflower Soup

Prepping: 5 Minutes
Cooking: 30 Minutes
Servings: 4

Calories: 45 Minutes
Carbs: 10g
Fats: 0g
Proteins: 3g

Ingredients
- Vegetable Broth (3 C.)
- Garlic Cloves (4)
- Onion (1, Chopped)
- Cauliflower (1/2 Head, Chopped)
- Salt (to taste)
- Dried Rosemary (1 t.)

Directions
1. This is a great recipe to have on hand because it only requires a limited amount of ingredients and time. When you are ready to make this soup, you will first need to cook the garlic and onion over medium heat. You will want to go ahead and cook these two ingredients for about five minutes before adding in the rosemary and cauliflower.
2. After another five minutes of cooking the cauliflower, add it in the vegetable broth to your pot and bring it to a boil. Reduce the heat once it is boiling and allow it to cook for about ten minutes.
3. You'll want to remove the pot from the heat after 10 minutes and allow it to cool down for about five minutes. When the liquid is slightly cooler, add it into your blender

and blend on high for thirty seconds. By the end, the soup should be nice and creamy looking.

4. If the soup is to your liking, pour into your serving bowl, top with some dried rosemary, and enjoy your soup.

Kale and Lentil Soup

Prepping: 10 Minutes
Cooking: 1 Hour
Servings: 4

Calories: 300
Carbs: 50g
Fats: 10g
Proteins: 15g

Ingredients
- Vegetable Stock (6 C.)
- Olive Oil (1 T.)
- Brown Lentils (1 C.)
- Onion (1/2 C., Chopped)
- Carrot (1, Chopped)
- Kale (5 C.)
- Harissa Paste (2 T.)
- Celery (1, Chopped)
- Salt (to Taste)
- Parsley (1/2 t.)
- Lemon (1/2, Juiced)

Directions
1. For a soup with a bit of a kick, you will absolutely want to give this recipe a taste! Begin by taking out a large pot and placing it over a low heat. As it begins to warm up, add in your olive oil along with the chopped celery, carrot, and onion. Once everything is in place, cook the vegetables for about ten minutes.
2. When cooking through the vegetables, add the paste, lentils, and the remaining seasonings. Take in the six

cups of vegetable stock with these in place and bring to a boil. Reduce heat once the soup is boiling and allow the soup to cook for about thirty minutes.

3. After thirty minutes, carefully add in the kale and allow the soup to cook for an additional twenty minutes. Once this time has passed, you can either leave the soup as is or place into a blender to make a creamier soup.

4. When you are ready to serve, pour the soup into your serving bowl, and carefully squeeze some lemon over the top.

Cheesy Broccoli Soup

Prepping: 5 Minutes
Cooking: 30 Minutes
Servings: 4

Calories: 200
Carbs: 20g
Fats: 10g
Proteins: 5g

Ingredients
- Olive Oil (1 T.)
- Vegetable Broth (3 C.)
- Garlic Cloves (2, Minced)
- Broccoli (4 C., Chopped)
- Onion (1, Chopped)
- Cooked Sweet Potatoes (1/2 C.)
- Cashews (1/2 C.)
- Nutritional Yeast (3 T.)
- Cayenne Pepper (1/2 t.)
- Salt (to Taste)

Directions
1. Just because you have gone plant-based, this doesn't mean you need to give up your cheesy broccoli soup! This recipe is plant-based friendly and acts as a healthier version of the classic soup.
2. To start out, you will want to take a pot and place it over medium heat. As it warms up, add in your olive oil and cook the onion for about five minutes.
3. Once the onion is cooked through, you will then add in the garlic, broccoli, and vegetable broth. Take the soup to

a boil with these in place, turn down the heat, and cook the soup at this lower temperature for five minutes.

4. As the soup cooks, it is time to make the "cheese" sauce! You can do this by placing the cashews into a blender along with a cup of water and blend until smooth. Once all of these ingredients are nice and smooth, add in the yeast flakes, onion, sweet potatoes, garlic, and some salt and pepper before blending again. When this is complete, remove from the blender and set it to the side.

5. Now that the broccoli is soft, you will want to take half of the soup and pulse it into the blender. Once that is set, place it back into your pot and stir before adding in your cheese sauce.

6. When everything is in place, cook for another five minutes or until the soup has thickened. When it reaches your desired consistency, remove from the heat and serve your soup up, hot!

Pesto Pasta Soup

Prepping: 5 Minutes
Cooking: 30 Minutes
Servings: 4

Calories: 300
Carbs: 50g
Fats: 5g
Proteins: 10g

Ingredients
- Vegetable Broth (4 C.)
- Olive Oil (1 T.)
- White Beans (1 Can)
- Gnocchi (8 Oz.)
- Zucchini (3 C., Chopped)
- Basil (1 C., Chopped)
- Garlic Cloves (3, Minced)
- Basil (1/2 t.)
- Oregano (1/2 t.)
- Cornstarch (1 T.)

Directions
1. Looking for something to warm you up? This soup will certainly do the trick! To start out, you will want to get your soup pot out and begin heating it over medium heat. As it warms up, toss in some olive oil and begin cooking the garlic and the zucchini pieces. After these have cooked for about five minutes, remove a cup of the zucchini before adding in the vegetable broth and herbs.
2. Turn the heat down to low once the soup starts to boil and let the zucchini simmer for about ten minutes. In the

meantime, you will want to get out a mixing bowl and combine one cup of broth with the cornstarch before adding into the rest of the soup. Once this is added in, be sure to stir the pot until the soup begins to thicken.

3. Once the soup is thickened to your liking, add in half of your basil leaves and then remove the pot from the heat. After the soup has cooled slightly, this is when you will want to place the ingredients into your blender and pulse until everything has become nice and creamy.

4. When the soup is to your liking, add it back into the pot over a low-medium heat. Once this is in place, add in the cooked zucchini that you saved from before along with the beans and the gnocchi. Once the gnocchi are cooked through, portion out into your serving bowls and enjoy!

Thai Noodle Soup

Prepping: 5 Minutes
Cooking: 20 Minutes
Servings: 4

Calories: 400
Carbs: 20g
Fats: 30g
Proteins: 5g

Ingredients
- Vegetable Broth (4 C.)
- Coconut Milk (1 Can)
- Garlic Cloves (1, Minced)
- Olive Oil (2 T.)
- Grated Ginger (1 T.)
- Rice Noodles (8 Oz.)
- Red Curry Paste (2 T.)
- Lime Juice (1 T.)

Directions
1. If you have a hard time choosing between soup or pasta, this recipe offers the best of both worlds! To begin this soup, you will want to get out a large pot and place it over medium heat. As it warms up, add in your olive oil, curry paste, ginger, and the garlic cloves. Go ahead and cook these ingredients for about two minutes or until you begin smelling the curry.
2. At this point, you will now need to add in the vegetable broth, a cup of water, and your can of coconut milk. With everything in place, go ahead and bring the soup to a boil.

3. Once the ingredients are boiling, you will add in your noodles and allow them to cook for three or four minutes. By the end of this time, the noodles should be soft.
4. When you are ready to serve your soup, portion into your serving bowls and gently squeeze some lime juice into each bowl. For additional garnish, feel free to add some green onions, red chilies, or even some crushed peanuts!

Roasted Herb Potatoes

Prepping: 10 Minutes
Cooking: 40 Minutes
Servings: 10

Calories: 130
Carbs: 20g
Fats: 5g
Proteins: 4g

Ingredients
- Olive Oil (3 T.)
- Baby Potatoes (3 Lbs.)
- Pepper (to Taste)
- Rosemary Leaves (1 T.)
- Salt (to Taste)

Directions
1. If you are looking for a basic side, these potatoes are easy to make but filled with flavor. You will want to start off by prepping the oven to 425.
2. As the oven heats up, get out your mixing bowl and baking sheets. Once the sheets are lined with foil and olive oil, take some time to chop your potatoes in half.
3. Once the potatoes are cut up, add it into your bowl along with the seasonings, rosemary, and a touch of olive oil. Be sure to toss everything together well to spread the flavor out.
4. When you are set, layer the potatoes across the pan and pop into the oven for fifteen to twenty minutes. After fifteen minutes, remove the potatoes from the oven and flip them all over. Once this step is complete, add the dish back into the oven and cook for another fifteen minutes.

5. By the end of this time, the potatoes should be golden, crispy, and ready to be served.

Lemon & Garlic Asparagus

Prepping: 5 Minutes
Cooking: 20 Minutes
Servings: 4

Calories: 60
Carbs: 10g
Fats: 5g
Proteins: 3g

Ingredients
- Asparagus (3 C.)
- Garlic Cloves (2, Minced)
- Lemon (1, Juiced)
- Salt (to Taste)

Directions
1. This recipe is perfect for serving as a side dish or even as a snack on hand! You will start by preheating the oven to 400 and lining your baking sheet with foil or parchment paper.
2. Next, you will want to take some time to trim your asparagus and then lay them evenly along the baking sheet. Once in place, carefully add the olive oil over the top along with the minced garlic and a sprinkle of salt.
3. Once the dish is set, you are going to pop the asparagus into the oven for twelve to fifteen minutes. By the end, the asparagus should come out tender.
4. For a final touch, juice the lemon over the asparagus, and your recipe will be set to be served.

Roasted Maple Carrots

Prepping: 5 Minutes
Cooking: 30 Minutes
Servings: 4

Calories: 100
Carbs: 20g
Fats: 5g
Proteins: 2g

Ingredients
- Olive Oil (1 T.)
- Carrots (3 C.)
- Maple Syrup (1 T.)
- Salt (to Taste)

Directions
1. If you have a picky eater in your home, these sweet carrots are the perfect way to sneak a vegetable onto any dish! Begin by heating the oven to 400.
2. As the oven warms up, you'll want to take this time to peel your carrots and then place them to the side. Once the carrots are set, you will take out a pan and place it over medium heat.
3. Once the pan is warm, you can add in your olive oil along with the carrots. When everything is in place, sauté the carrots for five minutes or until they are soft. At this point, you will want to lower the heat and add in the maple syrup. If you would like, you can also season with pepper and salt.
4. Now, get out a baking dish and line it with parchment paper. When your carrots are cooked nicely, toss them onto the dish and place it in the oven for another fifteen

minutes. By the end of this time, the carrots should be slightly browned and will be set for your enjoyment.

Chapter 7: Sauces and Dressings

Coriander Sauce

Prepping: 5 Minutes
Cooking: 0 Minutes
Servings: 4

Calories: 50
Carbs: 10g
Fats: 3g
Proteins: 5g

Ingredients
- Garlic Cloves (8, Minced)
- Green Chilies (4)
- Onion (1, Chopped)
- Coriander (2 C.)
- Salt (to taste)
- Water (1/3 C.)
- White Vinegar (1/4 C.)

Directions
1. Coriander is a nice sauce to have stored because it offers a fresh kick to any dish! To create this sauce, simply take the stalks off of your coriander, peel your garlic, and place everything into a blender for about thirty seconds.
2. Once the ingredients are combined, the sauce should look like a smooth paste. When it does, remove from blender and serve!

Simple Asian Sauce

Prepping: 5 Minutes
Cooking: 0 Minutes
Servings: 6

Calories: 10
Carbs: 3g
Fats: 0g
Proteins: 1g

Ingredients
- Water (1/4 C.)
- Soy Sauce (1/4 C.)
- Sugar (1/2 T.)
- Garlic (1 t., Minced)
- Lemon Juice (1 T.)

Directions
1. This sauce is great for dipping or over a salad! You will make this sauce by taking everything and placing it into your blender. You can adjust the sugar, and lemon juice amounts to your own taste.
2. When you are set, blend everything for a few seconds, and your sauce will be ready just like that.

Whiskey BBQ Sauce

Prepping: 5 Minutes
Cooking: 1 Hour
Servings: 1

Calories: 350
Carbs: 50g
Fats: 5g
Proteins: 5g

Ingredients
- Whiskey (1/3 C.)
- Pineapple Juice (1 C.)
- Ketchup (1 C.)
- Soy Sauce (1 T.)
- Molasses (1/4 C.)
- Cayenne Pepper (1/4 t.)
- Garlic Powder (1 t.)
- Onion Powder (1 t.)
- Salt (to Taste)

Directions
1. Nothing hits quite like a good BBQ sauce, but adding whiskey is a nice touch! To create this BBQ sauce, you will want to get out a saucepan and bring it over a medium heat. As it warms up, add all of the ingredients from the list above.
2. Once the sauce starts to boil, turn down the heat and allow it to cook for about an hour.
3. When the sauce is done, it can be served immediately.

Basic Pizza Sauce

Prepping: 5 Minutes
Cooking: 10 Minutes
Servings: 4

Calories: 140
Carbs: 20g
Fats: 5g
Proteins: 3g

Ingredients
- Tomatoes (1 Can, Crushed)
- Olive Oil (2 T.)
- Ground Fennel (1 t.)
- Garlic Cloves (2, Minced)
- Oregano (1 t.)
- Salt (to Taste)

Directions
1. If you are enthusiastic about your pizza, you already know that the sauce makes the difference between good and bad pizza! To create a simple pizza sauce, simply take all of these ingredients and mix them together in a bowl.

2. When these are set, you will want to add the sauce into a saucepan and simmer everything for about ten minutes. As the sauce simmers, before applying to your pizza dough, feel free to adjust any spices to your personal taste!

Kung Pao Sauce

Prepping: 10 Minutes
Cooking: 20 Minutes
Servings: 4

Calories: 150
Carbs: 15g
Fats: 10g
Proteins: 2g

Ingredients

- Garlic Cloves (2, Minced)
- Ginger (1 Inch, Minced)
- Olive Oil (3 T.)
- Water (2 T.)
- Vinegar (1 T.)
- Dark Soy Sauce (1/2 T.)
- Light Soy Sauce (1 T.)
- Peppercorn (1 t.)
- Cornstarch (2 t.)
- Sugar (1 t.)
- Green Onion (1 T.)
- Leek (2, White Part)
- Chili Pepper (6, Dried)

Directions

1. To begin this recipe, you will want to take some time to cut the white part out of your leek. Once this is done, you can cut the pieces into small circles and set to the side.
2. Next, it is time to get out your saucepan. As it warms up, add in some of your olive oil along with the peppercorn. Once you begin to smell the peppercorn, add in the dried

red pepper, garlic, green onion, and ginger. Be sure that you stir everything constantly and cook for an additional minute or so.

3. Finally, you will add in the rest of the ingredients. As the sauce begins to boil, turn the heat down to low and let everything simmer. After ten minutes, the sauce should be thick and will be set to be served over anything.

Lemon and Garlic Tahini Sauce

Prepping: 5 Minutes
Cooking: 0 Minutes
Servings: 1

Calories: 350
Carbs: 20g
Fats: 30g
Proteins: 15g

Ingredients
- Garlic Cloves (2, Crushed)
- Tahini (1/2 C.)
- Smoked Paprika (1/8 t.)
- Water (1/4 C.)
- Salt (to Taste)
- Lemon Juice (1/4 C.)
- Pepper (to Taste)

Directions
1. Tahini is an excellent sauce choice, whether you are looking for a salad dressing or a sauce for your veggies. To make this sauce, place everything in the list above into your blender and blend until combined well.
2. If you would like, you can add more water to thin the sauce out. Once it is to your liking, the sauce will be ready to be served instantly.

Greek Dressing

Prepping: 10 Minutes
Cooking: 0 Minutes
Servings: 4

Calories: 330
Carbs: 2g
Fats: 20g
Proteins: 1g

Ingredients
- Red Wine Vinegar (3 T.)
- Olive Oil (1/2 C.)
- Garlic Clove (1, Minced)
- Pepper (to Taste)
- Dijon Mustard (1/2 t.)
- Dried Oregano (1 t.)

Directions
1. As you begin a plant-based diet, you will want to avoid the processed salad dressing. Lucky for you, it is easy enough to make your own! For this basic salad dressing, whisk all of the ingredients above in a bowl, and you have Greek salad dressing within two minutes!

Sesame Salad Dressing

Prepping: 10 Minutes
Cooking: 0 Minutes
Servings: 4

Calories: 80
Carbs: 3g
Fats: 5g
Proteins: 1g

Ingredients
- Rice Vinegar (2 T.)
- Coconut Aminos (1/4 C.)
- Olive Oil (2 T.)
- Garlic Clove (1 t., Minced)
- Sesame Oil (1/2 T.)
- Medjool Dates (3)
- Ginger (1 t., Grated)

Directions
1. To create the base of this dressing, you will want to take some time to soak the dates in some hot water. Once they are soft, add them into the blender and blend on high for a few seconds. By the end of this time, the dates should be creamy.
2. Once the dates are done, add them from the list to the rest of the ingredients and pump the blender until they are mixed to your taste.
3. Now, you have dressing for your salad!

Spiced Ginger Salad Dressing

Prepping: 5 Minutes
Cooking: 0 Minutes
Servings: 4

Calories: 250
Carbs: 5g
Fats: 20g
Proteins: 1g

Ingredients
- Apple Cider Vinegar (2 T.)
- Maple Syrup (1 T.)
- Olive Oil (1/2 C.)
- Dijon Mustard (2 T.)
- Salt (to Taste)
- Ginger (2 t.)
- Pepper (to Taste)

Directions
1. Looking for a dressing with a fresh kick? This is the recipe for you! All you have to do is take a small mixing bowl out, combine the ingredients from above, and your dressing will be ready in an instant.

Poppy Seed Salad Dressing

Prepping: 5 Minutes
Cooking: 0 Minutes
Servings: 4

Calories: 300
Carbs: 15g
Fats: 25g
Proteins: 1g

Ingredients
- Poppy Seeds (1 T.)
- Apple Cider Vinegar (1/4 C.)
- Olive Oil (1/2 C.)
- Dijon Mustard (1 t.)
- Sugar (1/4 C.)
- Salt (to Taste)

Directions
1. To begin making this dressing, you will want to get out a mixing bowl and first combine the white sugar with the apple cider vinegar.
2. Once these ingredients are combined well, add in the salt and Dijon mustard. Now that mostly everything is in place, you will want to begin whisking your ingredients and slowly add in the olive oil.
3. Finally, pour in your poppy seeds, and your salad dressing will be prepared.

Chapter 8: Main Dishes

Ramen Veggie Pad Thai

Prepping: 5 Minutes
Cooking: 10 Minutes
Servings: 4

Calories: 350
Carbs: 40g
Fats: 20g
Proteins: 10g

Ingredients
- Ramen Noodles (2 Packages)
- Mixed Vegetables (2 C.., Frozen)
- Olive Oil (1 ½ T.)
- Peanut Butter (3 T.)
- Hot Water (2 T.)
- Teriyaki Sauce (1/4 C.)
- Sriracha (1/4 t.)

Directions
1. As you first start this dish, you will want to cook the ramen noodles according to the directions provided on the package. As you cook the noodles, you will want to leave the flavor packet out. When the noodles are cooked to your liking, place to the side.
2. Next, it is time to get out your large skillet. As you place it over a medium heat, add in the olive oil followed by the frozen vegetables. Go ahead and cook these for about five minutes or until the vegetables have thawed out.

3. When you are ready, get out a small mixing bowl so you can combine the sriracha, water, soy sauce, and the peanut butter. With this set, add the noodles into the saucepan and gently pour the sauce over the top.
4. Over a medium heat, continue to stir the ingredients together until everything is coated and hot. For additional flavor, portion out your meal and serve with some red pepper flakes sprinkled over the top.

Coconut Curry Chickpeas

Prepping: 10 Minutes
Cooking: 30 Minutes
Servings: 4

Calories: 400
Carbs: 40g
Fats: 30g
Proteins: 10g

Ingredients
- Coconut Milk (1 Can)
- Ginger (1 T.)
- Garlic Cloves (3, Minced)
- Coconut Oil (1 T.)
- Onion (1, Chopped)
- Crushed Tomatoes (1 Can, 15 Oz.)
- Curry Powder (1 T.)
- Chickpeas (1 Can, 15 Oz.)
- Spinach (4 C.)
- Optional: Fresh Cilantro

Directions
1. This dinner is awesome because it offers a lot of flavor and a boost of protein! To start off, you will want to take out your saucepan and begin heating the coconut oil over a medium heat. Once the oil is melted, place the chopped onion in and cook for five minutes. By the end of this time, the onion should be soft.
2. Next, you are going to add in the curry and ginger powder along with the minced garlic. Just cook these for one minute before adding in the coconut milk and the

crushed tomatoes. Once everything is in place, turn the heat up and bring everything to a boil.

3. When the ingredients begin boiling, turn the heat down instantly and allow the mix to simmer for ten minutes. At this point, you can season with anything you desire.

4. After ten minutes, add in the spinach and chickpeas. Once you have stirred the ingredients together, go ahead and cook everything for an additional five minutes.

5. When you are set to serve your meal, serve over a bed of rice or in a bowl! For extra points, garnish your dish with some freshly chopped cilantro.

Portobello Mushroom Steak

Prepping: 5 Minutes
Cooking: 30 Minutes
Servings: 4

Calories: 140
Carbs: 5g
Fats: 15g
Proteins: 2g

Ingredients
- Olive Oil (1/4 C.)
- Portobello Mushrooms (3)
- Steak Spice (4 T.)
- Salt (to Taste)
- Rosemary (1, Chopped)

Directions
1. While you may not be eating a traditional steak on a plant-based diet, these portobello mushroom steaks are pretty similar! You will want to start this recipe off by prepping the oven to 400.
2. As it warms up, take the olive oil and mix it with the steak spice and the salt. Once these are combined, go ahead and coat your portobello mushroom pieces and place onto a baking dish.
3. With this set, pop the dish into the oven for about thirty minutes. By the end, the mushroom caps should be cooked through and can be taken out of the oven.
4. For a full meal, serve the steaks with a side of roasted vegetables or even with some baked potatoes! As a final touch, add fresh rosemary and enjoy!

Sweet and Spicy Tofu Bites

Prepping: 20 Minutes
Cooking: 10 Minutes
Servings: 4

Calories: 150
Carbs: 8g
Fats: 10g
Proteins: 10g

Ingredients
- Hoisin Sauce (3 T.)
- Red Pepper Flakes (1/2 t.)
- Chives (1 T., Chopped)
- Firm Tofu (1 Block, Cubed)
- Olive Oil (2 T.)
- Soy Sauce (1 T.)

Directions
1. Before you begin this delicious recipe, you will want to take some time to press the moisture out of your tofu. By doing this, you will be able to get crispier tofu! Once this step is complete, place the tofu to the side.
2. Next, you will want to get out a mixing bowl so you can combine the soy sauce, hoisin sauce, red pepper flakes, and the chopped chives. When these are mixed well, add in your tofu and allow it to marinate in the flavors for twenty minutes.
3. When you are set to cook your tofu, take a pan and place it over a medium heat. As it warms up, you can drizzle in your olive oil and then   place the tofu in. Go ahead and cook the tofu for ten to fifteen minutes, or until it looks

nice and crispy. As you cook, the sauce will become sticky on the tofu.

4. Finally, remove the tofu from the stovetop and allow to cool slightly before serving.

Portobello Stroganoff

Prepping: 10 Minutes
Cooking: 50 Minutes
Servings: 2

Calories: 500
Carbs: 40g
Fats: 30g
Proteins: 20g

Ingredients
- Vegetable Broth (2 C.)
- Garlic Cloves (2, Minced)
- Portobello Mushrooms (3 C., Sliced)
- Oregano (1 T.)
- Onion (1, Diced)
- Rosemary (1 T.)
- Thyme (1 T.)
- Cashews (1 C.)

Directions
1. The first step for this recipe will be soaking your cashews. You can place them right into your blender with about a half of a cup of water.
2. While the cashews soak, you will want to get out a large pot and place it over a medium heat. Once warm, add in some olive oil along with the garlic, onion, and the mushrooms. Go ahead and cook these ingredients for about five minutes.
3. When the vegetables are cooked through, lower the heat and add in the two cups of vegetable broth. When the

ingredients begin to simmer, throw a lid on the pot and allow this recipe to simmer for thirty minutes.

4. After thirty minutes, go ahead and blend the cashews in your blender for several seconds or until it looks smooth. Once this step is complete, add it into the pot along with the herbs and begin stirring.

5. Now that everything is combined, you will want to leave the lid off and simmer the stew for an additional twenty minutes. As you watch the stew, feel free to add some water if the mixture looks too thick for your liking.

6. Finally, season your dish with some extra pepper and salt and serve over a bed of rice or pasta!

Chickpea Meatloaf

Prepping: 10 Minutes
Cooking: 1 Hour
Servings: 6

Calories: 200
Carbs: 30g
Fats: 5g
Proteins: 5g

Ingredients
- Panko Breadcrumbs (2 C.)
- Chickpeas (3 C.)
- Garlic Cloves (2, Minced)
- Onion (1, Diced)
- Carrots (2, Diced)
- Celery (1, Chopped)
- Soy Sauce (2 T.)
- Almond Milk (1/2 C.)
- Olive Oil (2 T.)
- Vegan Worcestershire Sauce (3 T.)
- Paprika (1 t.)
- Apple Cider Vinegar (2 T.)
- Tomato Paste (2 T.)
- Ground Flax Seed (2 T.)
- Maple Syrup (2 T.)
- Liquid Smoke (1 t.)

Directions
1. Meatloaf is a traditional dinner in many households. Now, you can make a healthier, plant-based version! To

begin, you will want to prep the oven to 375 and get a loaf pan ready by lining it with parchment paper.

2. Next, it is time to make the meatloaf. You will complete this task by putting together all of the ingredients into a food processor, including the vegetables, garlic, breadcrumbs, almond milk, flaxseed, tomato paste, soy sauce, olive oil, Worcestershire sauce, liquid smoke, and the pepper.

3. As you pulse all of these ingredients, you may need to work in batches. As you blend, be sure that the chickpeas are being broken down, but do not over process anything because it will become a mush!

4. Once you have your base set, press the mixture into the loaf pan you prepared before and pop the dish into the oven for about thirty minutes.

5. As the meatloaf portion of this recipe bakes, you can get your glaze together. You can do this in a small bowl; just mix together a ¼ of a cup of tomato paste, maple syrup, another tablespoon of soy sauce, 2 tablespoons of maple syrup, and 2 tablespoons of apple cider vinegar. For extra flavor, feel free to also sprinkle in some paprika!

6. After thirty minutes, remove the meatloaf from the oven and spoon your glaze over the top. Once it is covered completely, throw the dish back into the oven for an additional ten minutes.

7. Once the meatloaf is done cooking, remove from oven and allow the dish to cool for at least ten minutes before slicing it up and serving.

Kale and Sweet Potato Chili

Prepping: 10 Minutes
Cooking: 30 Minutes
Servings: 4

Calories: 150
Carbs: 30g
Fats: 5g
Proteins: 10g

Ingredients
- Olive Oil (1 T.)
- Sweet Potatoes (2, Cubed)
- Kidney Beans (2 C.)
- Kale (2 C.)
- Chopped Tomatoes (3 C.)
- Red Chili (1, Chopped)
- Garlic Cloves (2, Minced)
- Onion (1, Chopped)
- Ground Cumin (1 t.)
- Ground Cinnamon (1/2 t.)
- Salt (to Taste)

Directions
1. Chili is a great recipe to have on hand, especially on those harsh, cold days! To begin, you will want to get out a large saucepan and bring it over a medium heat. As it warms up, toss in some olive oil and begin cooking your garlic, onion, and cubed sweet potato. You will cook these ingredients for five minutes before adding in the spices and chili pieces.

2. After several minutes, add in your chopped tomatoes and kidney beans. Once these are coated well with the spices, lower your heat and allow the ingredients in your pan to simmer for about thirty minutes. If it becomes too thick for your liking, feel free to add in some water.
3. Now that the half-hour has passed add in the kale and allow it to wilt before you serve your chili. Be sure that you don't overcook the kale. Season with pepper and salt and your meal will be set.

Black Bean Burgers

Prepping: 10 Minutes
Cooking: 20 Minutes
Servings: 4

Calories: 120
Carbs: 20g
Fats: 5g
Proteins: 5g

Ingredients
- Instant Oats (1/3 C.)
- Ketchup (2 T.)
- Mustard (1 T.)
- Onion Powder (1 t.)
- Garlic Powder (1 t.)
- Black Beans (1 Can)

Directions
1. There are several ways to enjoy a burger on a plant-based diet. While this recipe is rather simple, it serves as an excellent base! You will want to begin this burger by prepping the oven to 400 and lining a baking sheet.
2. Next, get out the mixing bowl and begin mashing down your black beans. You can leave some bean parts, but they should be mostly pureed.
3. With the beans set, stir in the rest of the ingredients and blend well. Now that you have your mixture take your hands and shape patties and place them onto your baking dish.
4. When you are set, pop the dish into the oven for ten minutes. After ten minutes, the burgers should be browned on the edges and can be removed from the oven.

5. Now, build your burger as you normally would and enjoy your plant-based meal!

Mushroom Goulash

Prepping: 10 Minutes
Cooking: 50 Minutes
Servings: 6

Calories: 100
Carbs: 15g
Fats: 5g
Proteins: 5g

Ingredients
- Mushrooms (2 C.)
- Onion (1/2, Sliced)
- Olive Oil (2 T.)
- Red Pepper (1, Chopped)
- Thyme (6 Sprigs)
- Paprika (1 ½ T.)
- Garlic Powder (1 t.)
- Salt (to Taste)
- Diced Tomatoes (1 Can)

Directions
1. To begin, you will first take out a skillet and place it over a medium heat. As this warms, add in a tablespoon of the olive oil and begin cooking the onion for about five minutes. After this time has passed, add in the bell pepper and cook for an additional five minutes. Once these vegetables have been cooked to your liking, set them to the side.
2. Next, you are going to add in another tablespoon of olive oil and cook four mushrooms for three minutes. After three minutes, season with garlic and salt and cook for

another five minutes. Once the mushrooms are cooked, you can add the onion and pepper back in.

3. Finally, you will add the rest of the ingredients into your skillet and bring everything to a boil. Once boiling, reduce your heat to low and place a lid over the top. Go ahead and boil everything together for about twenty minutes, and then your dish will be set to be served hot.

Eggplant Casserole

Prepping: 10 Minutes
Cooking: 1 Hour
Servings: 4

Calories: 150
Carbs: 20g
Fats: 5g
Proteins: 5g

Ingredients
- Garlic Cloves (2, Chopped)
- Eggplant (2, Sliced)
- Diced Tomatoes (1 Can, 14 Oz.)
- Onion (1, Diced)
- Salt (to Taste)
- Parsley (2 T.)
- Cinnamon (1/8 t.)
- Red Chili Flakes (1/4 t.)
- Olive Oil (2 T.)

Directions
1. To make this recipe easier on yourself, it is beneficial to have a skillet that is ovenproof. When you are ready to get started, prep the oven to 350.
2. Next, you will want to prepare your eggplant by slicing it up and adding salt over the top. The salt will help draw out any excess moisture, so you don't have soggy eggplant!
3. When you are ready to cook, take out your skillet and place a layer of olive oil in the bottom. Once it is warm, begin frying the eggplant for about two minutes on either

side. If needed, you can cook in batches and use as much olive oil as you need. After the eggplant is golden, you can place it to the side.

4. Next, you will want to cook your onion and garlic for about five minutes in your skillet that has already been heated. After five minutes, add in your seasonings and tomatoes. Once these ingredients are in place, allow the mixture to thicken for five minutes.

5. With the sauce all set, you will carefully want to remove most of the sauce, leaving only a thin layer in the bottom. Then, you will layer your eggplant along the skillet and layer with sauce the way you would with a normal casserole.

6. Once the dish is set, cover with aluminum foil and place in the oven for about forty-five minutes. Once the sauce has reduced, remove the dish from the oven and allow to cool for ten minutes.

7. When you can handle the dish, cut your eggplant casserole up and serve with a fresh garnish of parsley.

Eggplant Lasagna

Prepping: 10 Minutes
Cooking: 3 Hours
Servings: 10

Calories: 200
Carbs: 10g
Fats: 15g
Proteins: 10g

Ingredients
- Olive Oil (4 T.)
- Egg Plant (3 ½ C.)
- Salt (2 t.)
- Whole Tomatoes (7 C.)
- Red Pepper Flakes (1/8 t.)
- Red Wine Vinegar (1/2 t.)
- Parsley (1 t.)
- Tomato Paste (1 T.)
- Garlic Cloves (2, Minced)
- Onion (1, Chopped)
- Capers (2 T.)
- Soft Tofu (2 Lbs.)
- Nutritional Yeast (3 T.)
- Lasagna Noodles (12 Ounces)
- Basil Leaves (1 C.)
- Lemon Juice (2 T.)
- Pepper (to Taste)

Directions
1. While this recipe does take several steps to make, the flavor is out of this world! Eggplant lasagna is the perfect

way to enjoy a dinner classic with less carbs! To start out this recipe, you will first want to cook the eggplant. To complete this task, prep the oven to 350 and begin slicing the eggplant lengthwise.

2. Once the eggplant is all sliced, go ahead and lay the pieces across a couple of baking sheets; if they are overlapping, that is perfectly okay! When the eggplant is in place, sprinkle the salt over both sides and allow this to sit for about thirty minutes to get the moisture out of the eggplant.

3. While you wait for the eggplant to dry out, you can go ahead and make the sauce for your lasagna. To do this, take out a food processor or blender and add in the tomatoes. Once the tomatoes are well blended, pop them into a large saucepan and bring everything over a medium heat for five minutes.

4. After five minutes, you can add in the garlic and the onion. With these items in place, cook for an additional three minutes before pushing everything to one side of the pan. When you have done this, place your tomato paste on the empty side and cook for two minutes before stirring everything together.

5. With all of these ingredients set, you will now add in the red pepper flakes, some salt, and the bay leaf. At this point, you will want to raise the heat until the sauce is boiling and then immediately reduce the heat, cover the pan, and simmer the sauce for forty-five minutes.

6. As a final touch for your sauce, you can add some capers for additional flavor and any other seasonings you would like. When the sauce is cooked through, place it in a bowl and set to the side.

7. Now that the sauce is done, it is time to finish your eggplant! After the time has passed, you may notice water beads have formed on the surface of your eggplant. Go

ahead and pat the eggplant down with some paper towels and then begin frying them in a pan over medium heat. Typically, it will take about five minutes on each side. As they cook, season with pepper and salt to your liking.

8. As the eggplant cooks, take a small bowl and mix together some red pepper flakes, vinegar, parsley, and two tablespoons of olive oil. Once you have stirred everything together, add it to your eggplant and toss well.

9. The next step for your lasagna will be to simply cook your noodles according to the directions provided on the package. When this is done, set the noodles to the side.

10. You are almost there! Now, it is time to make the tofu filling for the lasagna. When you are set, get your food processor back out and blend together the tofu with some lemon juice, pepper, salt, parsley, and the nutritional yeast. After you have blended for several seconds and it is smooth, set this to the side too.

11. Finally, it is time to assemble your lasagna! You will start off by lining your baking dish with some tomato sauce in the bottom. From there, you will add a layer of noodles and top with your tofu filling. Next, layer your eggplant slices over the top and spread some more tomato sauce. Go ahead and layer until you run out of room or ingredients!

12. When you are ready to cook your lasagna, cover the baking dish with some foil and pop into the oven for an hour. After an hour, remove the tin top and bake for an additional ten minutes. Once you are ready to serve your dish, garnish with some fresh basil and enjoy your masterpiece!

Lentil Tacos

Prepping: 10 Minutes
Cooking: 20 Minutes
Servings: 4

Calories: 250
Carbs: 40g
Fats: 5g
Proteins: 15g

Ingredients
- Corn Tortillas (4)
- Vegetable Broth (1/4 C.)
- Onion (1, Diced)
- Garlic Cloves (2, Minced)
- Cooked Lentils (1 C.)
- Olive Oil (1 T.)
- Ground Cumin (1 t.)
- Chili Powder (1 T.)
- Paprika (1/2 t.)
- Garlic powder (1/2 t.)
- Dried Oregano (1/4 t.)
- Salt (to Taste)
- Taco Toppings: Lettuce, Guacamole, Vegetables, Salsa

Directions
1. Yes, you can still have tacos on your new diet! You will start this recipe off by taking out a frying pan and cooking your onion over a medium heat with some olive oil. After they have cooked for five minutes, you can add in all of the spices from the list above along with the garlic.

2. When these are all set, add in the vegetable broth and lentils. At this point, you will want tog et out a potato masher so you can begin to mash the lentils. By the end, the lentils should look a lot like ground meat! After you have completed this step, allow the lentils to cook out the vegetable broth.
3. Finally, remove the lentils from the heat and build your tacos like you normally would!

Chickpea Burgers

Prepping: 10 Minutes
Cooking: 40 Minutes
Servings: 4

Calories: 120
Carbs: 20g
Fats: 5g
Proteins: 5g

Ingredients
- Carrot (1, Grated)
- Chickpeas (1 C.)
- Garlic Cloves (3, Crushed)
- Onion (1, Minced)
- Spinach (3 C.)
- Peanut Butter (2 T.)
- Soy Sauce (2 T.)
- Hot Sauce (1 t.)
- Nutritional Yeast (1 T.)
- Cumin (1 t.)
- Chickpea Flour (1/2 C.)

Directions
1. If black bean burgers aren't appealing to you, there are several other ways to enjoy burgers on a plant-based diet! Luckily, this one is packed with vegetables and is very healthy. To start out, you will want to cook your garlic and onion over a medium heat for about five minutes.
2. When the onion is soft, add in the carrot, spinach, and chickpeas. As you cook these ingredients, be sure to stir continuously, so nothing burns to the bottom of your pan.

Once all of the vegetables are soft, turn the heat off and dump them into a mixing bowl.

3. Now, you will want to add in the peanut butter, cumin, soy sauce, nutritional yeast, flour, and the hot sauce. When everything is cool to the touch, use your hands to create patties from the mixture.

4. When you have your patties, place them back into your pan and cook for five or six minutes on both sides. By the end, the burger should be crispy, and then you can build the burger as per usual!

Peanut Butter Tofu Bowl

Prepping: 10 Minutes
Cooking: 30 Minutes
Servings: 4

Calories: 400
Carbs: 50g
Fats: 30g
Proteins: 25g

Ingredients
- Extra-firm Tofu (16 Ounces)
- Olive Oil (2 t.)
- Spinach (2 C.)
- Cooked Brown Rice (2 C.)
- Carrots (2 C., Shredded)
- Broccoli (1 C.)
- Chickpeas (1 C.)
- Peanut Butter (1/4 C.)
- Maple Syrup (1/4 C.)
- Toasted Sesame Oil (2 T.)
- Chili Garlic Sauce (2 t.)
- Soy Sauce (1/4 C.)

Directions
1. Buddha bowls have been growing in popularity because they are filled with nutrients, flavor, and they are pretty to look at! Before you begin building your own bowl, go ahead and prep the oven to 400.
2. As the oven heats, you will want to take the time to press the excess moisture from the tofu and cut it into cubes.

When this step is complete, lay the cubes across a baking sheet and pop into the oven for twenty-five minutes.

3. When the tofu is baking in your oven, you can use this time to make up the sauce. You can accomplish this task by placing the peanut butter, garlic sauce, maple syrup, sesame oil, and the soy sauce into a mixing bowl and blend until smooth.

4. When the tofu is finished cooking through, you will want to place it in a bowl along with half of the sauce so that the tofu can marinate. As for the other half of the sauce, toss the broccoli pieces in it and stick in the oven for twenty minutes.

5. After the tofu has marinated for at least thirty minutes, take a skillet and place it over a medium heat. Once warm, add in your tofu pieces and bake until the tofu becomes nice and crispy. Generally, this should only take you about five minutes.

6. Finally, it is time to build your buddha bowl! You will want to place your cooked rice in the bottom and layer the rest of the ingredients on top!

Chapter 9: Snack Recipes

Snickerdoodle Energy Balls

Prepping: 10 Minutes
Cooking: 0 Minutes
Servings: 20

Calories: 100
Carbs: 15g
Fats: 5g
Proteins: 3g

Ingredients
- Medjool Dates (1 C.)
- Ground Cinnamon (2 t.)
- Cashews (1 C.)
- Vanilla Extract (1/4 t.)
- Almonds (1/2 C.)
- Salt (to Taste)

Directions
1. These little snacks are great op hand because they offer a boost of protein and are easy to grab on the go! To start out, you will want to place your Medjool dates into a food processor and blend until the Medjool dates become soft and sticky.
2. Next, you can add the nuts and seasoning along with the vanilla extract and blend until completely combined.
3. Now that you have your dough use your hand to create bite-sized balls and place onto a plate. You can enjoy

them instantly or place them in the fridge for thirty minutes and wait for them to harden up a bit.

Baked Carrot Chips

Prepping: 10 Minutes
Cooking: 30 Minutes
Servings: 8

Calories: 100
Carbs: 12g
Fats: 8g
Proteins: 1g

Ingredients
- Olive Oil (1/4 C.)
- Ground Cinnamon (1 t.)
- Ground Cumin (1 t.)
- Salt (to Taste)
- Carrots (3 Pounds)

Directions
1. As you begin a plant-based diet, you may find yourself craving something crunchy. This recipe offers the best of both worlds by giving you a crunch and something nutritious to snack on. You can begin this recipe by heating your oven to 425 and setting up a baking sheet with some parchment paper.
2. Next, you will want to chop the top off each carrot and slice the carrot up paper-thin. You can complete this task by using a knife, but it typically is easier if you have a mandolin slicer.
3. With your carrot slices all prepared, next, you will want to toss them in a small bowl with the cinnamon, cumin, olive oil, and a touch of salt. When the carrot slices are well coated, go ahead and lay them across your baking sheet.

4. Finally, you are going to pop the carrots into the oven for fifteen minutes. After this time, you may notice that the edges are going to start to curl and get crispy. At this point, remove the dish from the oven and flip all of the chips over. Place the dish back into the oven for six or seven minutes, and then your chips will be set!

Sweet Cinnamon Chips

Prepping: 5 Minutes
Cooking: 15 Minutes
Servings: 5

Calories: 70
Carbs: 5g
Fats: 5g
Proteins: 1g

Ingredients
- Whole Wheat Tortillas (10)
- Ground Cinnamon (1 t.)
- Sugar (3 T.)
- Olive Oil (2 C.)

Directions
1. If you are looking for a snack that is sweet and simple, these chips should do the trick! You are going to want to start out by getting out a small bowl so you can mix the cinnamon and sugar together. When this is complete, set it to the side.
2. Next, you will want to get out your frying pan and bring the olive oil to a soft simmer. While the oil gets to a simmer, take some time to slice your tortillas up into wedges. When these are set, carefully place them into your simmering olive oil and cook for about two minutes on each side, or until golden.
3. Once the chips are all set, pat them down with a paper towel and then generously coat each chip with the cinnamon mixture you made earlier. After that, your chips will be set for your enjoyment.

Creamy Avocado Hummus

Prepping: 5 Minutes
Cooking: 0 Minutes
Servings: 4

Calories: 120
Carbs: 5g
Fats: 10g
Proteins: 1g

Ingredients
- Olive Oil (1 T.)
- Avocado (1)
- White Beans (1 Can)
- Cayenne Pepper (1/4 t.)
- Lime Juice (2 t.)

Directions
1. When you are looking for something smooth and creamy to dip your vegetables or chips in, this is the perfect recipe to give a try! All you will have to do is place the ingredients from the list above into the food processor and process until smooth.
2. Place the avocado hummus into a serving bowl, and you are ready to dip.

Cauliflower Popcorn

Prepping: 10 Minutes
Cooking: 0 Minutes
Servings: 4

Calories: 100
Carbs: 10g
Fats: 5g
Proteins: 5g

Ingredients
- Olive Oil (2 T.)
- Chili Powder (2 t.)
- Cumin (2 t.)
- Nutritional Yeast (1 T.)
- Cauliflower (1 Head)
- Salt (to Taste)

Directions
1. Before you begin making this recipe, you will want to take a few moments to cut your cauliflower into bite-sized pieces, like popcorn!
2. Once your cauliflower is set, place it into a mixing bowl and coat with the olive oil. Once coated properly, add in the nutritional yeast, salt, and the rest of the spices.
3. You can enjoy your snack immediately or place into a dehydrator at 115 for 8 hours. By doing this, it will make the cauliflower crispy! You can really enjoy it either way.

Banana and Strawberry Oat Bars

Prepping: 10 Minutes
Cooking: 1 Hour
Servings: 5

Calories: 250
Carbs: 50g
Fats: 5g
Proteins: 5g

Ingredients
- Rolled Oats (2 C.)
- Chia Seeds (2 T.)
- Maple Syrup (1/4 C.)
- Strawberries (2 C.)
- Vanilla Extract (2 t.)
- Bananas (2, Mashed)
- Maple Syrup (2 T.)
- Baking Powder (1 t.)

Directions
1. These oat bars take a few different steps, but they are a great snack to have when you are short on time! You are going to start off by making the strawberry jam for the bars. You can do this by placing the strawberries and two tablespoons of maple syrup into a pan and place it over medium heat. After about fifteen minutes, the strawberries should be releasing their liquid and will come to a boil. You will want to boil for an additional ten minutes.
2. As a final touch for the jam, gently stir in the one teaspoon of the vanilla extract and the chia seeds. Be sure

that you continue stirring for an additional five minutes before removing from the heat and setting to the side.

3. Now, it is time to make the bars! You can start this part out by prepping the oven to 375 and getting together a baking dish and lining it with parchment paper.

4. Next, you are going to want to add one cup of your oats into a food processor and blend until they look like flour. At this point, you can pour the oats into a mixing bowl and place in the rest of the oats along with the baking powder.

5. Once these ingredients are blended well, throw in the other teaspoon of vanilla, maple syrup, and your mashed bananas. As you mix everything together, you will notice that you are now forming a dough.

6. When you are ready to assemble the bars, you will want to take half of the mixture and press it into the bottom of your baking dish and carefully spoon the jam over the surface. Once these are set, add the rest of the dough over the top and press down ever so slightly.

7. Finally, you are going to want to place the dish into the oven and cook for about thirty minutes. By the end of this time, the top of your bars should be golden, and you can remove the dish from the oven. Allow the bars to cool slightly before slicing and enjoying.

PB Cookie Dough Balls

Prepping: 10 Minutes
Cooking: 0 Minutes
Servings: 8

Calories: 70
Carbs: 10g
Fats: 4g
Proteins: 4g

Ingredients
- Whole Wheat Flour (2 C.)
- Maple Syrup (1 C.)
- Peanuts (1/2 C.)
- Peanut Butter (1 C.)
- Rolled Oats (1/2 C.)

Directions
1. Is this recipe a snack or dessert? That is completely up to you! To start this recipe, you will want to get out a large mixing bowl and combine all of the ingredients from the list above.
2. Once they are well blended, take your hands and carefully roll the dough into bite-sized balls before you enjoy! For easier handling, you will want to place the balls into the fridge for about twenty minutes before enjoying.

Chapter 10: Desserts

Almond Millet Chews

Prepping: 15 Minutes
Cooking: 0 Minutes
Servings: 10

Calories: 100
Carbs: 15g
Fats: 5g
Proteins: 2g

Ingredients
- Millet (1 C.)
- Almond Butter (1/2 C.)
- Raisins (1/4 C.)
- Brown Rice Syrup (1/4 C.)

Directions
1. This dessert is perfect for when you want something small after dinner. You will want to begin by melting the almond butter in the microwave for about twenty seconds. When this step is complete, place it into a mixing bowl with the brown rice syrup, raisins, and millets.
2. Once everything is blended well, use your hands to roll balls and place onto a plate. If needed, you can add a touch more syrup to keep everything together. Place into the fridge for twenty minutes and then enjoy your dessert.

Simple Banana Cookies

Prepping: 5 Minutes
Cooking: 20 Minutes
Servings: 4

Calories: 250
Carbs: 30g
Fats: 10g
Proteins: 5g

Ingredients
- Peanut Butter (3 T.)
- Banana (2)
- Walnuts (1/4 C.)
- Rolled Oats (1 C.)

Directions
1. For a simple but delicious cookie, start by prepping the oven to 350. As the oven warms up, take out your mixing bowl and first mash the bananas before adding in the oats.
2. When you have folded the oats in, add in the walnuts and peanut butter before using your hands to layout small balls onto a baking sheet. Once this is set, pop the dish into the oven for fifteen minutes and bake your cookies.
3. By the end of fifteen minutes, remove the dish from the oven and allow them to cool for five minutes before enjoying.

Basic Chocolate Cookies

Prepping: 5 Minutes
Cooking: 15 Minutes
Servings: 10

Calories: 100
Carbs: 10g
Fats: 5g
Proteins: 5g

Ingredients
- Cocoa Powder (1/2 C.)
- Almond Butter (1/2 C.)
- Bananas (2, Mashed)
- Salt (to Taste)

Directions
1. These chocolate cookies are a great way to get a touch of sweetness without overdoing the calories! To begin, prep the oven to 350.
2. As that heats, take out a mixing bowl so you can completely mash your bananas. When this is complete, carefully stir in the almond butter and the cocoa powder.
3. Once your mixture is created, place tablespoons of the mix onto a lined cookie sheet and sprinkle a touch of salt over the top. When these are set, pop the dish into the oven for about fifteen minutes.
4. Finally, remove the dish from the oven and cool before enjoying.

Quick Brownie Bites

Prepping: 10 Minutes
Cooking: 0 Minutes
Servings: 10

Calories: 150
Carbs: 15g
Fats: 10g
Proteins: 5g

Ingredients
- Cocoa Powder (1/4 C.)
- Medjool Dates (10)
- Vanilla Extract (1 t.)
- Walnut Halves (1 ½ C.)
- Water (1 T.)

Directions
1. to be honest, who isn't guilty of eating cookie dough raw? Now, you can do it on purpose! To begin this recipe, you will first need to get out a food processor so you can break down the Medjool dates. Once these are broken down, add in the rest of the ingredients and blend until combined.
2. Now that you have your batter, roll it into small balls, and your dessert is ready in an instant!

Peach Crisp

Prepping: 5 Minutes
Cooking: 15 Minutes
Servings: 2

Calories: 110
Carbs: 20g
Fats: 5g
Proteins: 2g

Ingredients
- Rolled Oats (2 T.)
- Flour (1 t.)
- Brown Sugar (2 T.)
- Peaches (2, Diced)
- Sugar (1 t.)
- Coconut Oil (3 t.)
- Flour (3 t.)

Directions
1. This recipe is built for two! You can begin by prepping the oven to 375 and getting out two small baking dishes.
2. As the oven begins to warm, take one of the mixing bowls and toss the peach pieces with the sugar, cinnamon, and a teaspoon of flour. When this is set, pour the peaches into a baking dish.
3. In the other bowl, mix together the three teaspoons of flour with the oats and the sugar. Once these are blended, pour in coconut oil and continue mixing. Now that you have your crumble, place it over the peaches in the baking dish.

4. Finally, you are going to pop the dish into the oven for fifteen minutes or until the top is a nice golden color. If it looks finished, remove and cool before slicing your dessert up.

Chocolate Dessert Dip

Prepping: 10 Minutes
Cooking: 0 Minutes
Servings: 6

Calories: 150
Carbs: 15g
Fats: 10g
Proteins: 5g

Ingredients
- Date Paste (1/2 C.)
- Cocoa (1/4 C.)
- Cashew Butter (1/2 C.)

Directions
1. Do you need to whip up dessert quickly? This is an excellent recipe to have on hand, especially if you want to impress your guests! All you have to do is place the three ingredients into a food processor and mix until blended.
2. Simply place the dip into a serving dish, and you are ready to go.

Lemon Coconut Cookies

Prepping: 15 Minutes
Cooking: 0 Minutes
Servings: 4

Calories: 450
Carbs: 30g
Fats: 20g
Proteins: 10g

Ingredients
- Coconut Flour (1/3 C.)
- Shredded Coconut (1 ½ C.)
- Agave (6 T.)
- Almond Flour (1 ½ C.)
- Lemon Zest (1 T.)
- Lemon Juice (4 T.)
- Coconut Oil (1 T.)
- Vanilla Extract (2 t.)
- Salt (to Taste)

Directions
1. If you enjoy dessert but are looking for something that isn't chocolate, this recipe will be perfect for you! To make these incredible cookies, you will want to place all of the ingredients from the list, minus the shredded coconut, into the food processor, and blend until you have created a dough.
2. Once your dough is set, take your hands and roll the dough into small, bite-sized balls.

3. As a final touch, roll the balls in your shredded coconut and then place into the fridge for twenty minutes. After this time has passed, go ahead and enjoy your dessert!

Watermelon Pizza

Prepping: 15 Minutes
Cooking: 0 Minutes
Servings: 4

Calories: 50
Carbs: 10g
Fats: 3g
Proteins: 1g

Ingredients
- Watermelon (1, Sliced)
- Banana (1, Sliced)
- Blueberries (1 C.)
- Coconut Flakes (1/2 C.)
- Chopped Walnuts (1/4 C.)

Directions
1. This dessert is pretty simple, but it can be a lot of fun to make and eat if you have kids in the house! You will begin this recipe by taking the watermelon and chopping it up to look like pizza slices.
2. When the watermelon slices are set, you can then add the chopped fruit on top of the watermelon, followed by any chopped nuts and coconut flakes. For this recipe, we chose to use bananas and blueberries, but you can use any fruit that you like!
3. Just like that, you have watermelon pizza for dessert!

Chapter 11: Three Week Meal Plan

Now that you have a good idea of the foods you will be able to enjoy on your new, plant-based diet, it is time to make a plan! After all, what good is a diet if you are just going to go into it blind?

The first step I invite you to take while creating your own meal plan will be choosing your goals. As you ponder this over, take into consideration your personal health when planning your personal goals. You will want to set goals for yourself that are achievable.

Unfortunately, in the modern world, it has become all too easy to compare ourselves to those we see on social media. However, it should be noted that just like you, these people are only posting the good! The fitness models you see aren't posting the struggle it took to get to where they are now. You will be witnessing the struggle firsthand, but with practice, it will become easier. All it is going to take is a plan!

Now that you have your goal, go ahead and write it down on a piece of paper that you are going to be able to see every day. Whether it be on your fridge, your mirror, or on your table, your goal needs to be visible so that it is always on your mind. It is going to take baby steps to get there, but with hard work and dedication, you can accomplish anything!

The meal plan to follow is going to be very basic to adhere to a number of different types of people. When you set your goals, you may have to alter this meal plan or even create one of your own! This meal plan is set to help individuals transition easily into a plant-based diet and does not take into account the number of calories nor macronutrients you need as an individual. The sole intention is to show you just how delicious and versatile your meal plan can be! When you are ready, let's get started!

Week One

As stated earlier, slow and steady will help you as a beginner. There are many people who jump in head-first with excitement and find themselves drowning later on. Instead, we are just going to dip our toes in for this first week.

Your goal for week one is to change at least one meal to a plant-based meal. This may seem like a small task, but changing our habits isn't as easy as one may think. Your body is literally addicted to the chemicals found in processed foods, and you are going to find yourself craving the foods. The good news is that you can change these cravings to whole foods, it is just going to take some time.

For the purpose of this meal plan, we are going to start off with breakfast! Breakfast is an important meal because it sets the tone for the rest of the day. If you eat healthy first thing in the morning, the hope is that the trend will follow through the rest of the day.

Here is an example meal plan:

Week One

Sunday	Monday	Tuesday	Wednesday
Green Machine Smoothie	Spinach and Carrot Cakes	Green Machine Smoothie	Basic Breakfast Hash Browns
Thursday	**Friday**	**Saturday**	
Good Morning Detox Smoothie	Spinach and Carrot Cakes	Basic Breakfast Hash Browns	

Shopping List

Fruits

- Pear
- Cucumber
- Pineapple
- Lime
- Mango
- Lemon
- Raspberries

Vegetables

- Spinach
- Onion
- Potatoes
- Carrots
- Kale

Baking Supplies

- Mint Leaves
- Agave
- Corn Flour
- Chili Powder
- Ginger Root
- Olive Oil

Other

- Orange Juice

As far as lunch and dinner go, you can either choose from the recipes in the chapters above or plan something very simple. An easy go-to lunch could be building a colorful salad! Once you have your base, feel free to add as many vegetables as you would like! Remember to go easy on the nuts, seeds, and the salad dressing. These items are the ones that will build up, calorie-wise.

Week Two

Congratulations on making it to week two! Before we jump into the meal plan, take a few moments to note how the first week went for you. Did you cave to your cravings? Did you stick to your meal plan? Either way, go ahead and give yourself a pat on the back! The point is, you are putting forth effort for your health, and for many, that is the hardest step!

Now that you have a better idea about the plant-based diet, it is time to take your meal plan one step further. This week, we will be including breakfast and lunch! Breakfast is generally pretty easy for people because it requires a small amount of time, and individuals are typically home for this meal. Lunch can get a bit more complicated.

Sunday	Monday	Tuesday	Wednesday
Oatmeal and Berry Smoothie	Cinnamon Roll Oats	Oatmeal and Berry Smoothie	Scrambled Tofu
Quinoa and Apple Salad	Basic Cauliflower Soup	Quinoa and Apple Salad	Basic Cauliflower Soup

Thursday	Friday	Saturday
Oatmeal and Berry Smoothie	Cinnamon Roll Oats	Scrambled Tofu
Sweet and Spicy Tofu Bites	Basic Cauliflower Soup	Sweet and Spicy Tofu Bites

With that in mind, you will want to think about your personal schedule. When it comes to lunchtime, will you need to plan ahead, or will you have time set aside to create lunch? These are all things to think about when you are following any diet. Yes, it takes a bit of effort to begin, but eventually, it can save you time and money!

Shopping List

Fruits

- Banana
- Strawberries
- Apples

Vegetables

- Carrots
- Mixed Greens
- Onion
- Cauliflower

Baking Supplies

- Rolled Oats
- Vanilla Extract
- Agave
- Ground Cinnamon
- Brown Sugar
- Olive Oil
- Nutritional Yeast
- Garlic Cloves
- Ground Cumin

- Parsley
- Dried Rosemary
- Hoisin Sauce
- Red Pepper Flakes
- Soy Sauce

Other

- Almond Milk
- Extra-firm Tofu
- Quinoa
- Walnuts
- Apple Chutney
- Vegetable Broth
-

If you find that you do not have time to make lunch, you have a few different options! The first option will be to stick with a basic salad or soup. These recipes take only a few minutes to make and can be prepared the night before, so all you have to do is pack and go! The second option would be eating leftovers from the dinner before! Eating leftovers can save you time and money because you won't be wasting any food.

During this second week, you will want to start taking a look at your lifestyle choices. Yes, a diet is going to help you get healthier, but being healthy is more than just what you are putting in your mouth. Are there other changes you can make to help you along your health journey?

One thing you may want to take a look at is your exercise routine. Do you exercise on a regular basis? If you don't, that is okay! There is no reason for you to jump into a cross-fit class right this minute. Instead, consider taking a light stroll around the office or grabbing a friend to go on a walk with. As long as you are moving your body to some capacity, that is a step in the right direction!

Week Three

You have made it to the final week! I hope that at this point in your diet, you are beginning to feel some major changes in your health. When people first begin a plant-based diet, they find themselves losing weight instantly! Often times, this is going to be excess water that your body has been holding onto, but as long as you stick to the diet, you will be burning off that excess fat before you know it!

In this final week, we are going to put everything together. Your challenge for this next week is to take the time for yourself to cook these delicious meals. While some may look at cooking as a torture device, it is all about your mindset! Cooking for yourself shouldn't be a downfall. Instead, think of using this time to enhance your health and enjoy the ability to fuel yourself with healthy and delicious foods!

Breakfast

As you go off on your own, you will want to keep your schedule and time management skills in mind. While breakfast is the easiest meal for some people, you may not have the time to spend on making a fancy breakfast, and that is okay! For this reason, I suggest making a batch of something at the beginning of the week or stick with a simple smoothie. Smoothies are great because you can have the ingredients on hand, throw them into a blender, and you have breakfast in an instant. You can also prepare smoothies by placing all of the ingredients into a freezer bag and having everything together when you need it! Either way, you have to do what works best for you!

Sunday	Monday	Tuesday	Wednesday
Crumble Apple Muffins	Creamy Orange Smoothie	Crumble Apple Muffins	PBC Breakfast Smoothie

Thursday	Friday	Saturday
Crumble Apple Muffins	Creamy Orange Smoothie	PBC Breakfast Smoothie

Shopping List

Fruits

- Banana
- Apple
- Orange

Baking Supplies

- Almond Meal
- Rolled Oats
- Brown Rice Flour
- Coconut Sugar
- Flaxseed Meal
- Baking Powder
- Vanilla Extract
- Cardamom
- Cocoa Powder
- Peanut Butter

- Almond Milk

Lunch

Next, we move onto lunch. As noted earlier, lunch can take a few different paths, depending on your schedule. Many people work and find it hard to make time for a healthy meal. As long as you plan ahead, you should have no issue sticking to your diet! Sure, McDonald's looks tempting, but that life is behind you now! Instead, make a plan, and look forward to the delicious whole foods you can prepare yourself!

Sunday	Monday	Tuesday	Wednesday
Cheesy Broccoli Soup	The Ultimate Crunch Salad	Cheesy Broccoli Soup	The Ultimate Crunch Salad

Thursday	Friday	Saturday
Kale and Lentil Soup	Cucumber and Chickpea Salad	Kale and Lentil Soup

Shopping List

Fruits

- Cucumbers
- Tomato
- Lemon

Vegetables

- Broccoli

- Onion
- Sweet Potatoes
- Radishes
- Cabbage
- Chickpeas
- Kale
- Celery
- Carrots

Baking Supplies

- Olive Oil
- Cayenne Pepper
- Nutritional Yeast
- Cashews
- Garlic Cloves
- Vegetable Broth
- Dill
- White Wine Vinegar
- Lemon Juice
- Parsley
- Brown Lentils
- Harissa Paste

If you find yourself truly short on time, remember that you can't go wrong with having dinner leftovers for your lunch! In week three, we will now begin planning for dinner, as well. With that in mind, you will want to choose dinners that have some of the same ingredients as your lunches. For this reason, you may want to keep your recipe selection very simple. This way, you aren't spending a fortune at the grocery store, and you will already have everything you need on hand at home!

Dinner

Last, but not least, it is time to start incorporating dinner into your meal plan! Hopefully, by week three, you are feeling more comfortable about the foods you can and cannot eat while following a plant-based diet. The thing is, we make a lot of meal choices throughout the week. The goal of creating a meal plan is to help take the thinking part out of making decisions. When you set a plan, all you will have to do is follow your shopping list, cook the meal, and enjoy! By following a plan this way, hopefully, it will help you stick to your goals!

Sunday	Monday	Tuesday	Wednesday
Chickpea Meatloaf	Build-your-own Salad	Black Bean Burgers	Build-your-own Salad

Thursday	Friday	Saturday
Coconut Curry Chickpeas	Build-your-own Salad	Mushroom Goulash

Shopping List

Fruits

- Crushed Tomatoes
- Diced Tomatoes

Vegetables

- Chickpeas
- Carrots
- Celery

- Mixed Greens
- Black Beans
- Spinach
- Mushrooms
- Onion
- Red Bell Pepper

Baking Supplies

- Panko Breadcrumbs
- Garlic Cloves
- Soy Sauce
- Almond Milk
- Olive Oil
- Vegan Worcestershire Sauce
- Paprika
- Apple Cider Vinegar
- Ground Flaxseed
- Tomato Paste
- Maple Syrup
- Liquid Smoke
- Instant Oats
- Ketchup
- Mustard
- Onion Powder
- Garlic Powder
- Coconut Milk
- Ginger
- Curry Powder

When you are planning out dinners, try not to get too complicated! If you are not enjoying the process, you are not going to stick to your diet. This is a trap that many individuals fall into and end up cheating on and eventually ditching their diet altogether! Do not be this person! You can follow a plant-based diet; it is just going to take some work.

As far as snacking and dessert go, that is completely up to you! When you begin a plant-based diet, you may be surprised to find how full you are going to be when you are eating whole foods. If your goal is to lose weight, remember that the calories you burn will have to exceed the number of calories you take in. This meaning, if you want to lose weight, you should consider cutting snacks and desserts.

Of course, it is okay to treat yourself once in a while! The desserts included in this book are on the healthier side and follow a plant-based diet. If you do want to include dessert in your meal plan, I suggest only indulging once or twice a week. The key here is to enjoy anything in moderation. If you feel you can find that balance, have at it!

Chapter 12: Tips and Tricks for a Plant-based Diet

At this point, you have probably noticed that there is a lot of buzz based around a plant-based diet, and it is for a good reason! But just like with any diet that you try, it can be extremely overwhelming when you are trying to figure out where to start.

I hope that you use this book to help build your foundation of knowledge before you begin your journey. As stated earlier, the key to a successful plant-based diet is having the information and putting it to good use. You can read about the diet all you want, but until you start taking action, you won't get the benefits!

To help you along the way, you will now read some of my favorite tips and tricks of getting started on a plant-based diet. As you begin to create a new lifestyle for yourself, you can apply these tricks but also build some of your own that fit your lifestyle! Remember that there is no right way of following a diet; you have to make it work for yourself.

Find Your Motivation

Just like with anything else in life, there needs to be a reason behind your actions. Before you begin your diet, ask yourself what your motivation is. Some different reasons people begin this diet is for health-based concerns, while others want to help the environment or animals.

If you need help finding your motivation, you should try reading a book or watching a documentary based around the plant-based diet. Here, you can find solid, science-based evidence that shows you why eating plant-based can change your life and the world we live in. At the end of the day, education is going to be key.

Transition and Swap

As you begin your diet, you may find yourself saying, "Oh, I can't eat that," a lot to yourself. As you transition into a plant-based diet, you will want to try to make the swaps, slowly. When you swap out one animal product for a plant-based product at a time, it will make the process easier on your mind.

One of the hardest items for people to give up is dairy. The good news is that there are many alternatives on the market, as mentioned in the earlier chapters! Whether you like coconut, cashew, or almond, why not give them all a try! Eventually, you will land on one that you really enjoy, and it will make replacing dairy that much easier.

Have Staples

There are going to be times in your life where you simply just don't have the time to cook a fresh meal. Unfortunately, this is where a lot of people crash and burn on their diet and begin making excuses to eat junk again. This is where staple meals can come in handy!

No, you won't want to eat the same three meals for the rest of your life, but it is always a good idea to have some basic meals on hand when you are in a pinch. Whether this meal is a vegetable stir fry, a smoothie, or a basic salad, you will want to try your best to keep the ingredients in your home so you can whip up a meal without thinking twice about it.

Clean the Cabinets and Fridge

As you first transition into a plant-based diet, you will want to change your environment as well. Before you even begin the diet, you will want to go through the cabinet and fridge and get rid of anything that isn't plant-based. By doing this, you will be creating a clean slate for yourself. When you are no longer buying the junk food, you won't have it in the house to eat!

As you go through your kitchen, collect all of the food that does not belong on your new diet. You can choose to donate these foods to a local food group, give it to a friend, or just toss it! There is no reason to keep these goods just because you have already bought it. Today is a brand-new day, and you are not going to give in to temptation that easily!

Once you have a new slate, that will be the time for you to go grocery shopping. Before you hit the store, try to create a meal plan, so you aren't just buying random ingredients. Instead, you will walk in with meals in mind and will be able to buy fresh produce without any of it going to waste. If you have any questions about the staples you should have on hand, feel free to refer to the food-guide provided in the third chapter.

Prepare for Anything

Many of us do not have the luxury of a lot of time on our hands. For this reason, you will want to have plant-based foods ready to run with you. When we are on the go, it can be difficult to stick to any diet. So, instead of reaching for something that is highly processed, you will want to always have some type of snack in your bag or in your car with you.

Luckily, there are many different delicious options. In the 9th chapter, you will find a number of different snack foods that can be made in an instant and are small enough to grab and go. If none of these work, fresh fruit is always a great option! Either way, if you prepare and plan, nothing can stand in your way.

The same goes for planning your meals. When you start making your own meal plans, you will want to choose a day that you can sit down and take some time for yourself. Sometimes when we are in a rush, we don't put the effort a plan really needs, and then the whole plan falls apart. You can avoid this by setting your plan up on a day that you aren't as busy. This way, you can take a look at your schedule and plan for the whole week!

Find a Community

While following a diet is fun by yourself, we are generally impacted by those who surround us. If you have family members questioning the way you are eating, you may feel pressured to fall back into your own habits. If you feel alone, there are plenty of people out there who are trying to better their health, just like you!

An excellent place to start finding your plant-based tribe would be the internet! As you research the plant-based diet, you will find many groups who talk about their delicious plant-based life and all of the details that go with it. Whether you are looking for recipes, a place to rant about the diet, or have questions about the diet, a plant-based community will always have your back because they know exactly what you are going through. The goal here is to surround yourself with like-minded people to keep you on track.

Have Fun and Commit

The reason that so many other diets fail is because it becomes a prison for most people. There are diets on the market that are so restrictive; it is almost impossible to follow in the long-run. This is where the plant-based diet is different.

The plant-based diet isn't about restricting or torturing yourself. It may seem like it at first, but the goal is to help you create new habits, so you feed yourself with better nutrition. Along the way, you must remember to be kind to yourself. You are not going to reach your goals overnight! When you feel like you are failing or that you're not following the meal plan perfectly, there is no reason to beat yourself up. Step by step, keep your dreams in mind and continue working toward them. You would be amazed at how much your perception makes an impact on your reality. What it all comes down to is your commitment to yourself.

The only way to truly commit to anything in life is if you enjoy it! The next time you go grocery shopping, I want you to take some time to slow down and pay attention to all of the different foods that you will be able to enjoy on your new diet! Unlike other diets, there really aren't any restrictions. On a plant-based diet, there are still plenty of different vegetables, fruits, and beans for you to try. In fact, I bet there are some foods that you have never considered before!

A fun challenge for yourself as you begin a new diet is to try new recipes. Within the chapters of this book, you will find over seventy different recipes that offer all different types of flavors, textures, and nutrients. At no point should you feel like you have nothing to eat. There is a world of foods out there for you to try; it is up to you to put forth the effort and give them a taste!

Now that you have reached the end of this book, I hope that you have found this information both beneficial and informative. Starting anything new can seem scary, but eventually, it will become second nature to you! As long as you have your health goals in mind, nothing should stop you from reaching them.

Conclusion

Thank you for making it through to the end of *The Beginner's Guide to Plant-based Diet*, let's hope it was informative and able to provide you with all of the tools you need to achieve your goals whatever they may be.

Starting a new diet is a very worthy goal, but along the way, you should anticipate some challenges heading in your direction. When it comes to changing eating habits, this is often easier said than done! There are specific guidelines to follow in order to get the best results. With that in mind, remember that there truly is no reason to change everything at once. As you begin to change your diet and take baby steps, the weight will come off slowly but surely, and you will begin to feel more energetic and healthier.

Your one main goal for this entire time will be trying your best! You have now been handed many delicious recipes and a three-week meal plan; use it! If the meal plan doesn't mesh well with your lifestyle, you can make your own! You can honestly make as many excuses as you would like, but until you make the changes, you won't see the changes!

As you become accustomed to your new diet, remember to be kind to yourself. You will want to set realistic goals for yourself and take baby steps toward those goals. If and when you slip up along the way, try your best not to punish yourself. However, it is important that you don't stray away for too long. We all make mistakes! Instead, start fresh for your next meal. There is never a big enough reason to fall off the bandwagon completely. So, what if you ate something that wasn't plant-based? It really isn't the end of the world! Get right back on that horse and continue eating right!

Finally, if you found this book useful in any way, a review on Amazon is always appreciated!

I hope you find your healthy journey to be prosperous and life-changing, and I wish you the best of luck along the way!

If you liked this book and you want more delicious plant-based recipes, you can also buy my second book "Plant-based cookbook for beginners"!

Made in the USA
Monee, IL
31 July 2020

37351164R00105